Growing up before Stonewall

It is easy to forget what it must have been like in "the old days" to grow up with sexual and emotional feelings that were different. This book tells the stories of eleven American gay men who tried to understand their identities in the years before the modern gay liberation movement began. From the 1920s through the 1960s, from a variety of regions and social classes, the men describe their families, early childhood sexual experiences, "coming out" in settings unlike the gay neighborhoods and communities of today, and their current romantic and sexual lives. For some men the military presented the opportunity to explore their personal and social identities; while for others, a chance encounter in a seminary, an accidentally discovered gay bar, or a heterosexual marriage provoked them into exploring deeper needs and desires. The variety of experiences illustrates the numerous ways individuals come to know their gay selves in an often unfriendly and hostile world. Interviews with a contemporary elder of the gay movement and a heterosexual psychiatrist, instrumental in arguing against categorizing homosexuality as a mental disorder, supplement the original eleven stories. Enlightening, sensitive and entertaining, the collection will be a landmark work in the growing field of gay and lesbian writing.

Peter M. Nardi is Professor of Sociology, Pitzer College, Claremont, California. **David Sanders** is Emeritus Attending Psychiatrist at Cedars-Sinai Medical Center in Los Angeles and Associate Clinical Professor of Psychiatry at the University of California, Los Angeles. **Judd Marmor** is Franz Alexander Professor Emeritus of Psychiatry at the University of Southern California and Adjunct Professor of Psychiatry at the University of California, Los Angeles.

Growing up before Stonewall

Life stories of some gay men

Peter M. Nardi, David Sanders
and Judd Marmor

London and New York

First published 1994
by Routledge
11 New Fetter Lane, London EC4P 4EE

Simultaneously published in the USA and Canada
by Routledge
29 West 35th Street, New York, NY 10001

Typeset in Times by Michael Mepham, Frome, Somerset
Printed and bound in Great Britain by
Mackays of Chatham PLC, Chatham, Kent

British Library Cataloguing in Publication Data
A catalogue record for this book is available from the British Library.

Library of Congress Cataloging in Publication Data
has been applied for

ISBN 0–415–10151–4 (hbk)
ISBN 0–415–10152–2 (pbk)

Contents

About the authors

Peter M. Nardi, Ph.D. is Professor of Sociology at Pitzer College, one of the Claremont Colleges located near Los Angeles. He completed his doctorate at the University of Pennsylvania and his undergraduate degree at the University of Notre Dame. He has written many articles for academic publications on such varied topics as magic and magicians, men's friendships, anti-gay hate crimes and violence, the social impact of AIDS, and alcoholism and families. He edited *Men's Friendships* (1992, Sage Publications) and a special issue of *California Sociologist* on "The Social Impact of AIDS." He is politically active in the gay community, having served as chair of the Sociologists' Lesbian and Gay Caucus of the American Sociological Association, co-chair of the Los Angeles Gay Academic Union, and as co-president and board member of the Los Angeles chapter of the Gay and Lesbian Alliance Against Defamation (GLAAD).

David Sanders, M.D. is Emeritus Attending Psychiatrist at Cedars-Sinai Medical Center in Los Angeles and Associate Clinical Professor of Psychiatry at the University of California (Los Angeles). He was Director of Residency Training and Acting Director of the Department of Psychiatry at Cedars-Sinai Medical Center. In private practice for over thirty years, he is a Life Fellow of the American Psychiatric Association and has written many scientific papers on various psychiatric and public health issues.

Judd Marmor, M.D. is Franz Alexander Professor Emeritus of Psychiatry at the University of Southern California and Adjunct Professor of Psychiatry at the University of California (Los Angeles). He is a former President of the American Psychiatric Association and of the American

Academy of Psychoanalysis. Among over 300 scientific publications, he has written *Modern Psychoanalysis* (1968) and *Psychiatry in Transition* (1974), and edited *Sexual Inversion: The Multiple Roots of Homosexuality* (1965) and *Homosexual Behavior: A Modern Reappraisal* (1980).

Acknowledgments

Assistance in preparing the manuscript was provided by Sandy Hamilton, Sean Martinez, and Lin Morris. We also give special thanks to Jim Moore who, when money for a project like this was impossible to obtain from the usual grant sources, helped with a generous gift to do a pilot study. Ultimately, this led to Dr. Marmor obtaining a grant from the National Institute of Mental Health. The Pitzer College Research and Awards Committee provided a small grant for manuscript preparation and transcription.

Introduction

In 1973, the American Psychiatric Association took the position that homosexuality was not by itself a mental illness. This view, however, was not shared by many of its members. Some 40 percent of the full membership did not agree with the conclusions of the scientific committee, despite convincing research from Evelyn Hooker (1957), who confirmed what many had thought for years: that there was no essential difference in the psychopathology of homosexual and heterosexual men.

In the late 1970s, Los Angeles psychiatrists Judd Marmor and David Sanders thought that there was need for further confirmation of the Hooker results, inasmuch as large numbers of practicing psychoanalysts, psychiatrists, and psychologists still took the view that homosexuals who came for treatment ought to be helped in changing their sexual orientation. They treated the problems that homosexuals presented as if the problems were caused by their homosexuality, rather than assuming that their sexual orientation was an independent, coincidental finding. Homosexuality was viewed as the pathology, as if it were unrelated to social conditions and attitudes of the time.

It was Marmor's and Sanders's hypothesis that the anxiety, depression, or schizophrenia that their gay and lesbian patients exhibited was not influenced by their sexual orientation. They had much anecdotal clinical evidence that the very people who viewed themselves as helping their patients were unwittingly hurting them. These therapists did not believe that homosexuality was compatible with a reasonably healthy and productive life.

In view of this, Drs. Marmor and Sanders decided to see if they could find evidence to support the Hooker view in individual psychiatric interviews. Their original plan was to match two groups of vocationally successful men who had never had psychotherapy: one heterosexual group and one homosexual group. The aim was to gauge the quality of their lives, the differences between the two groups in their life histories, and to see if there was any difference in the perceived degree of psychopathology.

The gay interviews were conducted in New York, Washington, San Francisco, and Los Angeles in 1979 by David Sanders. The subjects were recruited by colleagues and friends. Both the recruiters and the subjects were told that this was a psychological study of vocationally successful men, focusing on the factors that led to success and the difficulties they faced. They also were informed that the study would consist of a prolonged interview, a Rorschach Test, and a thematic apperception test.

An interview schedule was developed by Marmor and Sanders, covering a variety of issues ranging from relationship with parents, to early childhood social memories, adolescent and early adult sexual events, and current personal and professional information. However, the interviews were conducted primarily using a free-association technique. If at the end of the interview Sanders found that certain topics had not been covered, he went back to these topics and asked specific questions.

The eleven homosexual men who were interviewed all grew up before the Stonewall rebellion of 1969, before the gay liberation movements of the 1970s and 1980s, and before AIDS. These were men who tried to find their identity in the days when police regularly raided gay bars and baths; men who worked in environments where they would be fired if they were discovered to be homosexual. It was also a time, however, when sex itself was relatively risk-free.

After the interviews were edited in 1983 by sociologist Peter Nardi, they seemed dated in the face of a growing health crisis affecting similar gay white men in the same large, urban American cities in which these interviewees lived. There was very little interest in the data at the time, as academics, researchers, and the gay media began to turn their collective attention and skills to uncovering the story and causes behind the emerging AIDS pandemic.

Then, in 1991, Routledge published *Between the Acts: Lives of Homosexual Men 1885–1967*, edited by Kevin Porter and Jeffrey Weeks. Here was a collection of interviews with older British gay men conducted in 1978 and 1979, but published over ten years later "because of a growing interest in lesbian and gay history" and as "an unrepeatable source of evidence for a way of life that has now changed beyond recognition" (Porter and Weeks, 1991: vii).

While the life stories presented in this American version are not of men who grew up in the early part of this century, they are being published for the same reasons: to provide fascinating "insights into the complex, varied and uneven fashion by which homosexually-inclined people made sense of their needs and desires, and fashioned for themselves manageable social, and sexual ways of life" (Porter and Weeks, 1991: viii).

Although the people interviewed are all male and white, they tell many different stories about growing up and coming out in rural and urban areas, from the 1930s through the 1960s, in different parts of the United States, from varied social classes, and from several white ethnic and religious backgrounds. These interviews, of course, do not represent the much wider diversity of lives that exist among lesbian and gay people. However, the interviews should be of interest to people today and give a view of the social history and the psychology of homosexual men of that period.

In order to provide a sharper focus on the social and psychological context in which the eleven interviewed men grew up and came out, Part I includes two additional chapters and two new interviews. The first chapter (written by Nardi) provides a brief look at the social world that gay men faced in the years before Stonewall. It was an era of clandestine encounters, furtive glances, and moments of political consciousness as gay men and women began to transform what was viewed as both a medical and social stigma into a more positive sense of self and collective political identity.

To provide a first-person account of that era, this chapter is followed by an interview (conducted in January 1993 by Nardi and Sanders and edited by Nardi) with Los Angeles political and social activist, Morris Kight. His story of that period is a good example of someone taking society's negative labels and using them as a way of arguing for and organizing social and political movements to change individuals' lives and society's institutions. Kight's ability to take the skills developed in antiwar movements and bring them to the emerging gay movement in the late 1960s is highlighted in his interview. As one of the founders of the world's oldest and largest gay and lesbian social services center, Kight is an excellent example of how oppression can be transformed into social activism.

Chapter 3 (written by Sanders and edited by Nardi) describes the psychological world that faced gays and lesbians during the years the interviewees were growing up and coming out. The story is told of what psychiatrists and psychologists were taught about homosexuality and how they treated their homosexual patients. This is illustrated with examples from Sanders's own education and experiences in therapy, and as a psychiatrist who treated many gay and lesbian patients.

An interview with Judd Marmor (conducted in January 1993 by Nardi and Sanders and edited by Marmor) provides further evidence of the struggle some heterosexual psychiatrists had in convincing others in the psychological and psychiatric professions that first-hand experience with gay and lesbian patients contradicted many widely held prejudices about them. Marmor tells the story of his successful attempt over twenty years ago to get the American Psychiatric Association to declassify homosexuality as a mental illness.

Part II, after a brief introduction to the nature and methodology of the biographies and life stories (writted by Nardi), presents the interviews with the eleven gay men. In order to protect their privacy, pseudonyms are used and identifying details have been altered, while preserving the original meanings and intentions.

Part I

Growing up before Stonewall

Chapter 1

The social and political climate for gay men

The emergence of a visible gay community and positive gay identity in the years since the Stonewall rebellion in 1969 has its roots in the early American homophile movements of the 1950s and 1960s. The institutional changes that had been occurring in the military, the psychiatric profession, and the criminal justice system since the late nineteenth century were also starting to affect homosexual behavior and identity. However, for many of the men and women growing up and coming out between 1930 and 1970, their lives were a constant negotiation between the forces of institutional oppression and domination and their own developing sense of self. What follows is a brief summary of the major historical accounts of the period during which the gay men in our study grew up and came out (in particular, Adam, 1987; Berube, 1990; and D'Emilio, 1983).

BEFORE WORLD WAR II

D'Emilio (1983) has argued that the conditions for homosexual identity to emerge were set when American society shifted toward industrial capitalism during the second half of the nineteenth century. The meanings of family and marriage were altered as agrarian people's survival increasingly became dependent on selling one's labor for wages. Cities developed and attracted ever-increasing numbers of people, especially those for whom autonomy and individualism were important characteristics. Soon, an independent personal life, particularly for men, was possible: "Affection, intimate relationships, and sexuality moved increasingly into the realm of individual choice, seemingly disconnected from how one organized the production of goods necessary for survival" (D'Emilio, 1983: 11). And for women, romantic friendships in the nineteenth century and an emerging lesbian subculture after World War I, developed from existing social networks (Faderman, 1991).

Thus, from the 1870s to the 1940s, in American cities, "a class of people [emerged] who recognized their erotic interest in members of their own sex, interpreted this interest as a significant characteristic that distinguished them from the majority, and sought others like themselves" (D'Emilio, 1983: 11). However, homosexual behavior was variously viewed as a sin, a serious crime, or a disease. The risk of arrest (and conviction of a felony) prevented a gay subculture and identity from emerging more openly among gay men and lesbians.

Some historical evidence exists about early gay subcultures. Chauncey (1985) describes the sexual culture in Newport, Rhode Island in 1919–20, surrounding the Naval Training Station. By this date, medical discourse had not yet affected the military hierarchy nor how working-class men categorized themselves and their identities. It is also clear from Chauncey's research that the criteria used to label people as sexual deviants in that period did not conflate homosexual identity and behavior as simply as is done today. How men varied from traditional gender roles may have been more relevant in categorizing "queer" behavior than the gender of the sexual partner (Chauncey, 1985).

Other pre-World War II evidence of an early form of gay subculture can be found in Chicago with the Society for Human Rights, the first formally organized gay movement group in the United States (inspired by the early 1900s German gay movement), which unfortunately folded soon after its founding in 1924 when its leader, Henry Gerber, was arrested and convicted (Adam, 1987).

For some time, the medical profession diagnosed homosexuality as an illness and a pathology, often defining homosexuals as people who exhibited characteristics of the opposite sex. The attempt to move homosexuals away from the scrutiny of the criminal justice system to the supposedly more humane care of the medical and psychiatric professions led to a major reconstruction of homosexuality: "homosexuality shifted from being an aberration for which individuals were punished to a condition that inhered in a person and defined one's very nature" (D'Emilio, 1983: 19). Although this medical model had not been widely accepted outside of academic and professional circles, it set the stage for the later emergence of gay identity: homosexuality could now be seen as part of one's nature and being, rather than an immoral impulse punishable by law.

However, finding gay life remained accidental. Self-hate, individual pathology, and the social hatred of medicine, law, and religion were commonplace and prevented most gays from gathering and seeking one another. Then, World War II created a context in which those already aware of their feelings, and those just coming to understand them, were put together and able to discover each other.

THE WAR YEARS

It was during World War II, in the military's attempt to deal with homosexuals more humanely, that imprisonment was replaced by psychiatric treatment, thereby reinforcing "the idea that homosexuals were sick people and that homosexuality itself was an illness" (Berube, 1990: 148). But the structure and organization of military life, ironically, provided many men and women with opportunities to explore their feelings and to experience more permissive sex and same-gender sexual behavior.

The ways in which gay men and lesbians were screened, discovered, and discharged allowed the weakening of "barriers that had kept gay people trapped and hidden at the margins of society" (Berube, 1990: 255). For the first time, as Berube uncovered, draftees were asked about their homosexual feelings, stereotypically effeminate men and masculine women were often assigned similar jobs, and a bureaucratic military apparatus was built to deal with homosexuals.

Psychiatrists were mobilized to search out a "homosexual personality type" that helped give gays and lesbians a new identity category. In 1940, influential psychiatrists Henry Stack Sullivan and Winfred Overholser mounted a campaign to promote psychiatric screening of potential inductees by the Selective Service System. Within a year, "homosexual proclivities" entered the list of disqualifying deviations: by mid-1941, "the administrative apparatus for screening out homosexuals at three examination points—the Selective Service System, the Army, and the Navy—was already in place" (Berube, 1990: 12).

This represented a significant shift from a theory that mental and moral abnormalities (such as homosexuality) were caused by hereditary neurological disorders or brain lesions, sometimes brought on by trauma or bad habits. Between the world wars, there developed a growing interest in personality theories and a view that homosexuals were psychopathic and distinguishable by stereotypical signs. Many were able to conceal their homosexuality and few were rejected (Berube, 1990).

Inadvertently, the military and psychiatric policies allowed gays and lesbians to see themselves as a class of people and to find each other. Some were thrown into psychiatric wards and stockades, where they united as victims of oppression. The stage was set for an emerging postwar mobilization and activism, and a developing gay subculture. As Berube (1990: 257) describes it:

> The proliferation of gay bars, the broadening of public discussion of homosexuality, the formulation of the idea that homosexuals constituted a minority, the widespread acceptance of the psychiatric model of homosexuals as sexual psychopaths, the emergence and growth of federal antihomosexual policies and bureaucracies, and the opening of new avenues through which gay citizens could appeal government injustices against them were some of the many legacies of World War II. These changes had a powerful impact on how a nation and its people would respond to homosexuality long after the war.

AFTER THE WAR

Even in urban areas where post-World War II life led to a growing gay subculture, the dominant ideologies constructed homosexuality as an individual perversion. To let these men and women know that they were not alone and that there were others like themselves became the first stages in the developing gay movement. But until that sense of group identity was established, the thought of leading a healthy life as a single gay person, or even "settling down" with a partner in a relationship not unlike heterosexual marriage, remained inconceivable. After all, the 1950s were the years of the prototypical "traditional American family" and any variations, even for heterosexuals, were impossible to imagine.

Hence, it was not uncommon to read in the early gay literature such questions as Cory (1951: 133) posed: "Is it possible or desirable for two people of the same sex to be in love with each other, just as a man is in love with a woman; to show the same affection and interest, to offer the same loyalty, to form a union as permanent?" Negative answers to this question often stated that it was not impossible, but that psychological and biological barriers were more likely to prevent love and commitment. The "nature" of gay men was seen to be promiscuous, due in part to the "scientific" belief in the inability of achieving real sexual pleasure with another man.

Although many gay men and lesbians found some sort of community in a few large urban centers, for many others, the "homosexual lifestyle" was a lonely, isolated experience filled with short-term sexual adventures, often out of sight from a legal spouse. A political concept of gay identity was only starting to develop.

Part of the process of creating identity was an attempt to get gays and lesbians to see themselves not in pathological individualistic terms, but as people who, when organized into some collective sense of identity, could have a happy and successful life just like heterosexuals supposedly had. What was needed was a shift from a sexual category to a human identity based on non-erotic ties, a collective culture with its own institutions and ideologies.

To achieve this, there was a need to develop understanding among gays and lesbians that they were an oppressed minority, imprisoned by the dominant heterosexual culture. For many in the 1950s, the debate to organize a "highly ethical homosexual culture" centered on assimilation: either to seek respectability within the framework of the dominant ideologies or to recreate alternative socio-political structures (D'Emilio, 1983).

But the official legal, political, religious, and mental health institutions' definitions and ideologies of homosexuality often were in opposition to what gay men and lesbians wanted and experienced in their lives. For people struggling to achieve a healthy and positive self-identity, the battles took their toll. Some sought relief in alcoholism, suicide, and repressive marriages, eventually seeking psychiatrists to help change them to heterosexuals. Others decided to act against the hegemonic definitions and organize resistance.

According to Adam (1987), the rise of a gay and lesbian movement has been a collective alleviation of antihomosexual practices and a challenge to domination. In America, the opposing forces during the post-World War II years included the injection of homosexuality into the rising anticommunist fervor of McCarthyism. Gays and lesbians, already bearing the label of mentally ill, would hear the National Chairman of the Republican Party say in 1950: "Perhaps as dangerous as the actual Communists are the sexual perverts who have infiltrated our Government in recent years" (quoted in Adam, 1987: 58).

Out of this suppression, circles of friends in large urban areas, such as New York, San Francisco, and Los Angeles, began to develop homophile support groups and discussion groups. Most notable was the Mattachine Society, created in the Silver Lake section of Los Angeles in 1951. This group—along with the earlier appearance of the Kinsey Report in 1948, publication of Cory's 1951 book *The Homosexual in America*, and even a 1951 California Supreme Court decision ruling that no state law prohibited gay people from gathering in bars—marked the beginnings of a growing social and political consciousness of gay identity and community (D'Emilio, 1983). Soon, a growing restlessness among other marginalized and powerless groups, especially blacks in the American South, led to challenges of the assimilationist model of resistance (Adam, 1987).

Some of this call to action can be heard in Cory's (1951: 25) plea:

the shame of belonging and the social punishment of acknowledgment are so great that pretense is almost universal; on the other hand, only a leadership that would acknowledge would be able to break down the barriers of shame and resultant discrimination. Until the world is able to accept us on an equal basis as human beings entitled to the full rights of life, we are unlikely to have any great numbers willing to become martyrs by carrying the burden of the cross. But until we are willing to speak out openly and frankly in defense of our activities, and to identify ourselves with the millions pursuing these activities, we are unlikely to find the attitudes of the world undergoing any significant change.

THE 1960s

On June 26 1964, *Life* magazine published "Homosexuality in America: The 'Gay' World Takes to the City Streets" (Welch, 1964). Other head-lines of the article included "rejected by the 'straight' world, homosexuals build a society of their own;" "in a constant conflict with the law, the homosexual faces arrest, disgrace;" and "a legal–religious debate grows over personal immorality."

Accompanying the article were photos of a leather bar where patrons "make a show of masculinity and scorn effeminate members of their world," a store front "filled with the colorful, off-beat, attention-calling clothes that the 'gay' world likes," "fluffy-sweatered young men," "fla-grant homosexuals," and other references to male prostitution, tight clothing, wearing women's clothing, and "when arrested for soliciting, he burst into tears." Such were the images, stereotypes, and the media's interpretation of gay life in America in the early 1960s.

Yet, the appearance of this article and other newspaper accounts had the effect of introducing the existence of a gay subculture to many, both gay and straight, who had not heard of it. A more public view of gay life was occurring, contributing to an evolving sense of self and community.

One example of the changing sense of identity and community can be found in the language used by gay men and lesbians to describe their relationships and friendships (see also Nardi, 1992; Weston, 1991). In postwar gay circles, the word "family" was almost exclusively limited to family of origin, as in Cory's (1951) use throughout his book. However, it was not uncommon then (and even today) for people to signal that others were also gay or lesbian by suggesting that they were "a member of the family," and sometimes with even more explicit kinship terminology. Warren (1974: 109–10) writes about the gay men she got to know in "Sun City's" already large pre-gay-liberation community from 1968 to 1973:

> several words used to describe community relationships are social kinship words like mother, auntie, and sister. ... Gay people are bound by bloodlike ties of fate and community as are aunts and nephews or mothers and sisters, and their sociable interaction has the same formal and obligatory character as visits from relatives.

Incest taboos among close friends were often stated in kinship terms, as in Rodgers' (1972: 181) definition of "sister" in his gay dictionary: "he will share anything but his bed with friends. A sister is sexually neutral with his comrades; he is a chum, not a lover. Sisters are in the same business, but only as competition." Other entries in the book include such terms as auntie, sugar daddy, brother, mother, mom, and daughter, some used by lesbians and others by gay men. For the most part, kinship terms were one way of signifying who were nonsexual, "just friends" in opposition to those who were "more than friends" in a sexual sense. This is evident in Crowley's (1968: 134) play, *The Boys in the Band*: "No man's still got a roommate when he's over thirty years old. If they're not lovers, they're sisters."

Along with this changing sense of community and subculture, social movements of resistance were emerging among women, blacks, and antiwar activists: "The proliferating social movements of the decade, which came to be known as the New Left, engendered a militancy in the gay community that overturned the homophile approach [of the 1950s]" (Adam, 1987: 68).

Before long, Frank Kameny's Mattachine Society chapter in Washington, DC, took a more aggressive position for gay rights, challenging various federal agencies about their discriminatory policies in 1962 and 1963. The New York chapter followed in 1964 with its election of more radical leaders; the Daughters of Bilitis, the San Francisco Society for Individual Rights, and other chapters of Mattachine soon found themselves reorganizing, reviving, and debating strategies and approaches. In 1966 there were fifteen gay and lesbian organizations; by 1969 there were fifty (D'Emilio, 1983). Yet most gays and lesbians still remained invisible and not part of the movements.

This ascendancy of a more activist and militant style in the late 1960s and the break from the more assimilationist approach of the 1950s made gays and lesbians more visible to the media and introduced the subculture to isolated homosexuals. As D'Emilio (1983: 174) describes it:

> The militants' rejection of the medical model, their assertion of equality, their uncompromising insistence that gays deserved recognition as a persecuted minority, and their defense of homosexuality as a viable way of living loosened the grip of prevailing norms on the self-conception of lesbians and homosexuals and suggested the contours of a new, positive gay identity. The militant viewpoint also made possible the adoption of tactics that widened the horizons of the movement and magnified the expectations of its participants.

Then, in 1967, several hundred people, the largest gay demonstration up to that time, protested the raiding of bars in Los Angeles. Two years later, on Friday evening, June 27, 1969, in Sheridan Square, at the Stonewall Inn on Christopher Street in New York City, Puerto Rican drag queens, lesbians, effeminate men, and young street people resisted a police raid and fought back. Two more nights of fires, hurled bottles and stones, and demonstrations followed.

By Sunday, the Stonewall Inn was burned, "Gay Power" graffiti appeared, and, within months, Gay Liberation Front groups starting forming throughout the country. One year later, between 5,000 and 10,000 men and women marched from Greenwich Village to Central Park. By 1973, there were over 800 gay and lesbian organizations in America.

When AIDS made its appearance in the early 1980s, a national gay infrastructure of organizations, media, neighborhoods, and economic and political clout contributed to a response that was needed in the face of indifference and opposition from official political, media, and medical institutions. The history of gays and lesbians and how they developed identity, community, and a social movement are stories still being uncovered and told. But, like the ones already described, they are also continuing stories of resistance, organization, and mobilization.

Chapter 2

Interview with Morris Kight

A pioneer of the gay liberation movements and a longtime Los Angeles activist, Morris Kight was born in Texas in 1919. From his earliest days at Texas Christian University (class of '42), he demonstrated his commitment to social justice by trying to racially integrate the school. Throughout the 1950s and 1960s, he became active with the NAACP (the National Association for the Advancement of Colored People), the Southern Christian Leadership Conference, and the National Mobilization Committee to End the War in Vietnam. He founded the Dow Action Committee (one of the first antiwar groups) in 1965 and was protesting the 1968 Democratic National Convention in Chicago with the Southern California antiwar delegation. His experiences and dedication to social reform shaped his involvement in the growing gay/lesbian movement in Los Angeles in the 1970s. He has served the Los Angeles gay communities in many capacities, principally as founder of the Los Angeles chapter of the Gay Liberation Front (1969), the Christopher Street West organization (1970), and co-founder of the Gay and Lesbian Community Services Center (1971)—the world's first and largest organization of its type. He also co-founded Van Ness Recovery House (1973), the Stonewall Democratic Club (1975), and the Gay and Lesbian Caucus/California Democratic Party (1977). Today, he is in his fourteenth year as a commissioner on the Los Angeles County Commission on Human Relations.

Question: Morris, start recollecting what it was like for you in the 1940s as you were starting to come out. What was it like then? Where were you? Tell us what the context was like as well as your own stories. Go back to the beginning—the 1930s and '40s and '50s.

Morris: I'm not sure how to phrase it, because there were various degrees of gayness. If you proclaimed gayness, which I think would have gotten

you killed, socially ostracized, or discriminated against in the 1930s and
'40s and maybe even the early '50s, you just couldn't do that. And yet we
were around in great numbers, as we are now. We say, "we are every-
where." So we had to find expression for that. We did find that in gay bars
and through social contacts.

I practiced male–male sexuality when I was in high school in Texas,
and I'm happy to say that I didn't have a trace of guilt feeling about that,
not a trace. Those were kind of happy affairs. Then I went to Texas
Christian University at Fort Worth in 1937 to 1941, and there I was
somewhat active as a gay person. And I use the word gay deliberately
because that was how I felt. I didn't feel particularly homosexual, I felt
gay. Those were satisfying relationships.

Question: Where did you meet these people?

Morris: That's hard to answer—in social situations, casually, at the
university. There were kind of indications, kind of signals, that you sent.
There was a language that went with the signals. The language would
often go around the word 'gay'—"what a gay tie you're wearing," "it was
a gay experience," "we went to the theater and it was so gay," and so on.
If after eight or ten or twelve such references, if the person didn't respond,
then you just assumed he wasn't understanding it. If he did respond, often
this led to a social contact and to a sexual liaison. It was tenuous and risky,
but often satisfying, if not thrilling.

There were gayish areas in Fort Worth where Texas Christian University is. There was a place downtown called the Southern Club, which had
a closeted gay clientele, but conversation between us would indicate some
level of gay consciousness and some frankness and some class difference.
We were kind of paired off by class. I was a part of that. It was risky
because I was an employee of the university. I was on the staff of the Dean
of Men and it was risky to be associated with gay people. There was a lot
of gossip and we were gossiped about. In the meantime I was in business
with my mother running a little cafe, a little tavern, just an inexpensive
little roadside place, and working there, and trying to keep up a fifteen-unit
course at the university, studying a lot, and having a wonderful time. So
I was practicing gayness, but I also knew that there were risks involved
in that. There was no real gay society. There were occasional gatherings
at the homes of people, but rarely were gay men affluent enough to
maintain their own apartment or home. They had to live with their families
and, of course, there are constraints on that. We practiced it, but there were
risks, and publicly it was a dangerous, criminal act.

Question: Had you ever thought about going to a psychiatrist? Didn't you hear that homosexuality was awful and pathological?

Morris: I had heard that all the time, but never, ever, for a moment in my life did I believe it or consider going to a psychiatrist. There was no reason to it. I didn't feel any guilt feelings of any kind and why pay a psychiatrist to go and say that you feel good about yourself. They're not in the business of hearing people who are happy; so why go. No, I never gave a moment's thought to it.

But I counseled people who were in trouble, got arrested or were in some form of danger, or people who were troubled about their gayness. I counseled them because I think I was really pretty good at that. As for me, I only had guilt feelings once in all those years of growth, and I think that's the word to use, because I'm still growing at the age of 73-plus. I'm still growing, I'm still evolving.

The first time I engaged in active anal intercourse with a man I had guilt feelings. I don't know where the conditioning came from; why oral copulation or "69"-ing didn't have a trace of guilt connection with it. Here was the first time I was actively intercoursing a man, and I did have guilt feelings about it for some little time. But I felt that under the theory that if you're thrown from a horse, get back on and ride again. It's known as the best cure to try again, so I attempted another active anal intercourse and it was thrilling and wonderful, and I felt why have I waited so long, and the rest is sexual history.

Many acquaintances of mine went to psychiatrists and concealed their homosexuality from the psychiatrist. They paid him/her money, good hard-earned money, to conceal the very thing that they went there to deal with in the first place. I never could understand the hypocrisy or cupidity of that. The psychiatrists were often much more sophisticated than their patients or clients. They had to cajole them into it, had to keep setting the stage to try to get you to proclaim your gayness.

After I left college in 1941, I lived in northern New Mexico, except for one brief interlude, until I came here in 1958. During that time there was an underground gay community in Albuquerque and particularly in Santa Fe. It was satisfying, but it was not totally pleasant. It was furtive. You'd gather at an apartment or a house for a beer party or a sex party or something or other. There was some lack of wholesome goodness about it, and being gay is really a wonderful experience. I guess I'm belittling the goodness of some of the people, but I didn't feel that we were really being honest with one another. But there were house parties, weekend parties, dance parties. There were three bars in Albuquerque that were gayish. They were hardly ever called gay bars. They didn't want to get themselves closed up, but they were gay bars. There was a social life there, a social order.

The police just winked them off. I think that in the southwest there was this kind of pioneer tradition where each pot kind of sits on its own bottom. The police didn't want to admit there was such a thing in the world and just paid no attention to the bars. However, if you publicly were caught or if you were enticed or entrapped, you suffered horridly.

One professor at the University of New Mexico, a distinguished man from a distinguished family, was heterosexually married, attempted heterosexual marriage, and at the same time was practicing underground gayness. One time, he was in the basement of the City Hall—a known cruising place to the cognoscenti, and which was also the jail in Albuquerque— and coming on to a 17 year old Hispanic. A police officer, who made it his main course of fare to spy on gay activity, was hidden in a kind of a window well and peering through the window and observing this activity and went and arrested them both. The professor got three years in the New Mexico State Prison and there did a very gay thing of organizing a school. As soon as he got there—and being brainy and bright—even though he was cowed from his horrible arrest, he had enough wherewithal to go to the prison authorities and convince them he could open a school in the prison. They encouraged that, and so he had college-level courses, high school and grade school classes, and English as a first language, and Spanish as a first language, and was just teaching all over the place. When he left they were very sad and held a ceremony for him and said they were sorry to see him go because he had created such a school.

There was not one trace of protest about the arrest, not one trace of any kind. Indeed, there was vicious gossip and non-objective newspaper reports, but I heard no really public, organized, liberal, progressive radical protest of any kind until the very late '60s. That really needs to be made clear. The pretense that there was a great movement is the worst historical revisionism and reconstructionism.

Question: Why do you say that? Wasn't the early '50s the beginnings of the Mattachines and One and other gay organizations and movements?

Morris: Well, in the first place they didn't call themselves gay, they called themselves homophiles. That's a perfectly good word. Indeed, I consider myself a homophile. However, I don't think they used the word homophile particularly because they were so enchanted with it intellectually. I think they used it as a scientific cover. There was not a movement. A movement means lots of people are aware, lots of people share, lots of people are personally motivated. There was not a trace of a movement. There was some organizing in major cities, largely a secret organization, often with pseudonyms, with a kind of Masonic mysticism of passwords, and a lot of medieval incrustation of just absolute pretentious nonsense. However, there were people who emerged from that who were doing research on what was called the "homophile condition" or the "homosexual condition."

But there were not all that many organizations in those days. In 1967, Foster Gunnison, a well-known man in research, published a newsletter for the North American Conference of Homophile Organizations (NACHO). He published a newsletter that contained eight and then nine and then ten and then fifteen organizations. It was so inexpensively made and in such limited quantity that it was printed on a hectograph—you know the gelatin with purple ink—and sent out. It was a daring effort.

I'd find the names of organizations listed in these newsletters and you could write and say "I'm a homophile or a just curious person and am interested in being on your mailing list, so send me things." There was correspondence among us, and that correspondence, while it's kind of exotic and rare, is all terribly valuable because much of it indicated an emerging consciousness that something could be better.

I was involved in theater for five years from 1950 to 1955. I just got into the theater because I felt that theater was a place where social consciousness could be inculcated, where there would be a chance to express oneself and meet some very pleasant people. So I associated with the Summerhouse Theater in Albuquerque, a professional training theater in the summers, which was headquartered in a building that I controlled.

It was an ancient building in the San Felipe Hotel, which was built in 1706. I had restored the hotel into a museum and art gallery and art center and garden. Summerhouse Theater was there in the summertime and Old Town Players were there in the winter, and I was involved with both. A number of those involved came from the California theater—we trained what are now some extraordinarily famous names, indeed a number of Academy Award winners have come out of those training schools. They commenced to bring in documents from California—Paul Coates's columns from the old *Los Angeles Mirror*. His column was constantly putting gays down, but was nonetheless interesting reading. They also brought in the *Mattachine Review* and there was cross-culturalization. So contact started among us. I tried to be very friendly with the homophiles, although I didn't really like what they were doing.

I wasn't in total admiration of what the researchers were doing because I thought it was trivial and peripheral, and I didn't think that it had much scientific validity. They were doing research on the "homosexual condition," who we are and what that means—it was perfectly legitimate. We still are asking who are we and what it means. Other than survival right now because of AIDS, it's the number one question—who we are and what does that mean. They were doing that then; we are doing it still.

What I thought was necessary was street action; having a certain desire to live, I was already involved in other radical activities opposing war, poverty, and racism, and so on and so forth. I was already demonstrating in the streets. I felt that the late '50s and early '60s were a poor time for us as lesbian/gay people to go in the streets, and instead I chose to be friendly with the homophiles. At the same time, parallel to that, there was no significant support from them to do hands-on, person-to-person service for troubled or in trouble homosexual persons.

In Albuquerque I saw more and more injustice against homosexuals. Many of us involved ourselves in the Stevenson 1 campaign in 1952 and the Stevenson 2 campaign in 1956. We involved ourselves so directly that there was a lot of gossip about us gay persons supporting Stevenson, and there was even worse gossip about him. Republicans infiltrated the Stevenson campaign and suggested that he was gay. The "lavender factor" was the phrase used by the Republicans.

The gossip about us was just so devastating that a newspaper reporter in Santa Fe, Will Harrison, the most political reporter in New Mexico, took us on in his column, "Under the Capitol Dome," about our flamboyant ways, our scandalous conduct and behavior, and so on. That, coupled with many other negative indicia, told me that something needed to be done. So in 1958 I came to live in Los Angeles permanently and have lived here ever since.

I had been coming to LA a lot and had come here more and more and enjoyed coming here very much. I found that it was just heaven. The gay life in Los Angeles was underground, except for an "in" and "knowing" crowd. It was a lot of fun, but I also found that the oppression was just devastating. I came here because I felt that a social revolution—I really was thinking that way, a non-violent social revolution—was necessary, but I felt also that the only way to do that was to get into a laboratory situation. A situation in which you could deal directly on an intimate basis with the community—either people troubled or in trouble, and thus build up a following, build up a lot of knowledge, to learn who to deal with in the Probation Department, who to deal with in the courts, which police officer might be more kindly, how to deal with a property owner, how to deal with an employer, how to deal with an employer in a negative situation.

So I conducted a one-person laboratory. Then as the '60s wore on, I commenced to pick up some followers; people who felt that what I was doing was just great, or at least good. Of the several thousand people whom I dealt with in Los Angeles, many only wanted to deal with me to get some degree of support and service and then to be gone.

When I came to Los Angeles I had several addresses, first at 143 North Hope St., where the Department of Water and Power now is—indeed the apartment I was in is where the elevator lobby is on the first floor. I paid $45 a month rent for a one-bedroom apartment. I couldn't afford that because I didn't want to work. I was perfectly employable, I had public administration credentials, a certificate in personnel administration and so on, but I didn't want to work because I wanted to serve the people. So I paid $45 a month rent and in trying to economize, moved to 341 South Hope, down the street four blocks, to where the First Interstate Bank is, indeed where the lobby on the first floor is, and I paid $35 a month for that. That included the utilities, except the telephone charges, which were enormous. Phone bills were so much more then than they are now. Making a long-distance call was like buying a newspaper ad. The $35 rent plus telephone, plus car, and gasoline was 18½ cents a gallon.

So to survive I took two sources of income. I worked for the Dodgers, the baseball outfit, as a novelty vendor out in front of the stadium selling program books and inexpensive novelties. I saw an ad in the *Los Angeles Times* that vendors were needed, and I thought that would be work that would be outdoors and the hours would not be all that much and I would still have lots of time to work with the people. I went down to the Coliseum, the back gate, and applied for the job. The man, an old pro at hiring people, said, "What do you know?" I said I knew Kaufman, I knew so-and-so—just tossing out names. He said, "Fine, you're hired." There were hundreds of people applying and only about twenty-five people hired. I set up my stand and he came along and could tell at a glance that I didn't have the slightest idea what I was doing. He could also tell at a glance that I was bright and alert and that I had an outgoing personality. He said, "I see that you don't know what you're doing, but let me help you out." In any case, I did that for four years and picked up some money from that. But even with that I was jealous of the hours because I had to give more hours to it than I wanted, and again I wanted to be serving the people.

Question: You get yourself an apartment, you get yourself a little job that barely pays for all of that, and you talk about serving the people. How did you find the people to serve or how did they find you?

Morris: It was the easiest thing in the world. I have a degree in personnel administration and public administration. I have a social service attitude. I believe in serving the people. When I would talk with people I would indicate that I was available for that and I gave out my telephone number, MA8–8610. Ultimately it was written over restroom walls.

Whatever it was people needed, I was able to get. Some of them would call and say, "They tell me that there is someone at the end of this phone who can help me, I'm in jail." I would say, "Yes, I can help you. Tell them nothing. Just give them your name and social security number, do not give them information of any kind, and I'll start to try and get you out of jail."

Then I would get an attorney and then I would provide counseling for them—here's how to deal with the Probation Department—and occasionally I would go to court with them to act in reassurance and sometimes appear as an expert witness. I know police and courts and parole an awful lot. As the word spread that I was nonjudgmental, nonthreatening, and nonexclusionary; as the word spread that I was skilled and knew what I was doing; as the word spread that I was nonoppressive in dealing with people; people enjoyed seeking me out. Ultimately, it became just enormous, hundreds of people a year, over a thousand in some years were seeking me out. Some of them to express the joy of being gay and others because I always took them.

As soon as I got off Bunker Hill, I took the biggest house I could find and I had parties and dances as an alternative to backseat or back alley or parks or washrooms or some such place. In the late '50s and early '60s, I had dances and parties, and big ones. Three hundred people came to my split-level house at 716 1/2 South Bonnie Brae in the Westlake Park district to dance on Friday, Saturday, and Sunday. The house had been custom built by a famous photographer of the great rich. The area had, from 1880 to 1935, grand houses, some three stories tall. The room I slept in had an indoor fountain/fish pond and an overhead glass roof with a huge window facing north. In the back was a granite stone wall, which reached far above the house and held back a street. It lent itself so well to big parties and group meetings. I paid $80 a month rent.

To pay for all this, I sold antiques. I was an arcane authority on antiques and so I would, for therapy, shop for antiques. Dealing with oppressed people constantly, dealing with people who are in trouble or troubled, can really negatively accumulate. So I would just flee and go to the thrift stores and garage sales and to the charity thrift shops and buy up the antiques. Since there were often people in the closet in those agencies who were aware of what I was doing, they would give me favors—"Oh, thank God you're here, I've gotten something hidden you won't believe." I went to one major charity thrift shop and one of the brothers said, "I could hardly wait for you to get here. I've been hiding it, hiding." He had a French hammered copper bathtub with four long wooden handles. The type that the several servants brought in for his lordship filled with reasonably warm water and soap, and then servants to bathe his lordship—a very valuable antique. He had hidden it away and I was able to get it for next to nothing and able to sell it for quite a little bit.

Every six months I held a sale. I developed a whole list of clients, among them Liberace, who came—he dealt in antiques, too, you may know—he came to buy and was as flamboyant buying as he was in his act. A lot of nongay dealers knew that I knew what I was doing. They would call and say, "Are you about ready to have a sale?" I would tell them I would have a sale in another month. There were a hundred of them or thereabouts, and I would call them and say, "I'm ready for a sale." They were terribly polite to me and I was exceedingly polite to them. They were very honest with me and I was very honest with them. I got things for next to nothing, sold them to these dealers for one-tenth or one-third of their value, and then they went and made a good deal of money on them.

Question: Meanwhile, the Mattachine Society had been started in LA. What was your relationship with them?

Morris: I knew that they were meeting. However, I was aware of their politics. First, they started out as a kind of replication of a European medieval order, secret password and a lot of nonsense that's not even fun mumbo jumbo. And then Hal Call came from San Francisco and out-maneuvered them and marched north to San Francisco expunging the socialists, communists, and radicals. Call came up with a loyalty oath and warped it into something of his own creation. I didn't think it was helpful. In the meantime, One had come out of Mattachine—I don't think they say that, I think One doesn't feel that they're an outgrowth of Mattachine.

Nonetheless, in 1952 it came about, and I was quite friendly with Don Slater, who was a full-time staff member of One. All those years we were quite friendly and I would counsel him and he would counsel me about how to do this, how to do that, I don't agree with this, I agree with that, and so on. So there was communication among us.

One had a Sunday afternoon social affair, gathering, which was terribly interesting. I went to those, partly to escape from the horrors of dealing with people in the streets who were troubled, because it was so serene over at 2256 Venice Boulevard, their headquarters on the second floor. It was just a serene place and there were lectures and conversation, largely white men, even though there's a pretense now that there were a lot of women involved, there weren't. At those affairs I heard Christopher Isherwood speaking, D. B. Vest, also known as Gerald Heard. He was into flying saucers and other exotic thought. I heard some of the great ones speak at those affairs. They were sparsely attended. I tried to be as friendly with them as possible while I was doing something else altogether. I was doing street organizing, street work, street counseling, one-to-one curbside counseling. Although I did see people in my home, people would be so troubled that they needed some quiet space. I would have them come to my house and sit and talk until they talked it out.

Question: At your parties and gatherings, was there now beginning a connection, a community, like "let's get politicized" or was it just socializing? Was there a lot of fear and anger? What was the mood?

Morris: Schizophrenia, and I don't mean as a mental illness, I just use it to describe the people who are of two parts—what one part wanted was to dance together, to have sex together, to drink together, to have fun together, to go to the beach together, to go to the mountains together; and then the other wanted to protect oneself from the public ridicule of coming out.

In 1962, I knew a man who worked in the film business. He worked for one of the distribution outfits, I think for 20th Century Fox, over on Vermont and Washington. It was called Film Row, where the bookings occurred. It was also, at least in part, a gay enclave of employment. He recognized he couldn't get promoted because they knew he was gay, and they felt they'd just have to put up with it. He wanted to break out of there, so he applied to the New York Life Insurance Company for a job as a junior accountant. He went and kept going for interviews. He kept coming back. I was counseling him about how to groom himself for the job. He came back for the fourth time and said, "Now I've been four times and they still are unwilling to commit themselves. They won't reject me, they won't accept me. I think it's because of my gayness." I said, "It could easily be, but you have nothing to lose because you're okay at Fox, they like you a lot and you can stay there as long as they last, so go back now and tell them." He said, "How do I do that?" I said, "Just sit in a chair, wrap both arms, and say 'is the reason why you're not hiring me because you suspect I'm homosexual' well, I am." And he practiced that. We engaged in role playing, and he got it in his head that he would do that.

So he went back over to their office on Wilshire Boulevard and came in and there were five men, all white European types, and he sat. They said they were still reviewing, then he said, "Is the reason why you're rejecting me because I'm homosexual and you figured it out?" "Good grief, we thank God, we thought you never would. We've driven ourselves crazy—is she or isn't she." It was easy—he said, "Look hon, we've driven them all out of here. We've made it so impossible they won't stay here. We've liberated the joint." So there were 150 gay men in an all-gay enclave typing it up for New York Life.

Let's take up another case. Irwin Harper was passing, not only as a gay person, but passing as an African American. His mother had been African American, his father had been European American. He had taken casual jobs in order to survive. So Doug Morden and I counseled him about getting a job with Continental Can Company, where there would be better working conditions and he could make serious money. We filled out an application form for him and sent it with him and counseled him on how to handle himself. He went to Continental Can over on 28th Street and applied. They started him out on the production line making cans. He couldn't do that, a whole week, he just couldn't do that. He kept ruining cans. Every week he'd come in and say, "They demoted me. They give me another job that's not as good as the job I had." The third week the personnel manager from Continental Can called and said, "Mr. Kight, this Irwin Harper whom you sent is not working out and I just need to tell you that we're going to have to let him go." He said, "We've tried him in everything and he simply cannot perform any job of any kind however menial it may be. I only have one question for you—is the man who's standing here the same person who was in the application form, because the application form seems to describe someone else totally different." I guess it did. We have to do the best we can, we have to get as many jobs as possible.

I think my major goal was for gay people to be proud of themselves. There was a way by which that was done and that was by what later on was called "rap groups." At a meeting at my house on Bonnie Brae in 1961, I said, "Everybody is gay, they just haven't found out yet." I think that was a prophetic statement. I wanted them to feel good about themselves. Next I wanted them to live lives of usefulness and creativity—to get a job, and income, and some stability, to have some savings, move up in the world, get a better apartment, and so forth. I wanted them to stay out of trouble. There were techniques by which you were able to do that. All the while I felt that was only patchwork to get ready for the revolution.

On New Year's Eve in 1967, on the eve of the inauguration of Ronald Reagan as California Governor for the first time, the Los Angeles Police Department (the LAPD), believing that Ronald Reagan would bring a new right wing, a kind of new crypto-fascism, believed that there would now be no restraints on the police of any kind. There weren't all that many restraints anyway, but now there would just be none. We had just gone through the Governor Edmund Brown, Sr. era, which was really terribly liberal and progressive. Governor Brown, Sr. said—in a radio address which drove LA Police Chief, William H. Parker, nearly crazy and had him holding press conferences—"I look forward to the time when police officers will not arrest or detain, they will counsel." Geez, that's a stunningly socially advanced position. It would still be a good idea. Chief Parker was screaming about that.

So, the police conducted a New Year's Eve raid in 1967 on a gayish bar over on Sunset and Sanborn in Silver Lake called The Black Cat. It's now called Basgo's. It had been a nongay go-go bar and when go-go went-went some gay people opened it up as a gay bar. The bar announced that it was having a New Year's Eve party, and a really good one. They were kind, decent, cheerful hosts and so a lot of people went to the New Year's Eve party. The LAPD were there dressed in gayish attire—they're very good actors.

Corduroy pants or chinos and desert boots that came just above the ankle, an interesting belt, not a big buckle, just an interesting belt, and a knit shirt, and a light jacket. That was the number one gay attire. The LAPD infiltrated the place and at midnight people started dancing and kissing, and a young man and a young woman started kissing. The police threw on the lights, leaped up on the bar and said, "This is a raid, freeze, you're all under arrest!" They arrested the man and the woman. Two other customers—not wanting to suffer the horror of an arrest, time in jail, and all that—went down the street to the northwest corner of Sunset and Sanborn to a gay bar called The New Faces. They fled there and the police chased after them. Here came the two men running with the police chasing after them. The door person, trained to keep people out who were troubled or drunk or whatever else, moved against all of this and was beaten up very badly by the LAPD. He wound up in the emergency ward at General Hospital—his spleen was ruptured, it had to be removed, and for three or four days he was on the critical list. Back at The Black Cat, nine people were arrested including the young man and young woman. She was arrested for being in drag, a man in woman's attire, when in fact she was a nongay woman. She was with her brother—there was understanding family then as there is now—and she wanted to spend New Year's Eve with him. The assault and the vulgarity of it all was such that I immediately launched a program to get them all out of jail. I was very good at that. Since I was part of a gay liberation underground—it really was a gay liberation underground, to pretend otherwise would just be foolish—we organized at my house.

In the meantime, other sectors of the community organized. There was a picket in Silver Lake beginning on Sunset, marching around the block from Lucille to Sanborn, then across Sanborn to Sunset and back. We went around with maybe seventy-five to eighty people—a lot of them, like me, radicals from other movements, and they were quite used to marching in the streets.

Silver Lake and Echo Park were a slight gay enclave, a slight gay ghetto in the '50s because they were close to Hollywood showbiz. With the red car you could get over here for a dime. That tradition had continued. It still does. There's still a gay underground in that area.

Question: You tell the story of your serving the people and it's very inspiring, but bad things must have happened to you while you were doing it. I wonder whether you can say a few words about that.

Morris: Yes, really horrible things happened to me. One winter in the early '60s, I was at Harold's, a famous gay bar written about in John Rechy's book *City of Night*, which he called Harry's. I was there one evening and I had just conducted an antique sale and had picked up $300. Foolishly, I had not gone to a bank to exchange the money, so I had three $100 bills with me—a lot of money for me. I went to Harold's and I had to exchange a $100 bill to get change, and Ronnie, the gay man who tended bar and kind of managed the place but hated himself desperately for being gay, saw that I had money and he finked on me to a hustler who had a reputation of jackrolling men—watching a man who's got some money on him. So this young man, terribly attractive, came on to me an awful lot and pandered to me. That was not unusual by the way—I was quite sexually active.

At about half past twelve he suggested we leave, and I said that my car was out front and I lived close by—I lived on Bunker Hill—and we could go there. He said, "Well, no, I live out in Huntington Park." So we went out into the parking lot to his car and when I got there the windows were darkened. He said, "I'll drive." When I got in there were two other people in the car—one a man over 21 and the other man less than 21. So there was me, and this man, and two more men, one under 21. He sped out of the parking lot in a big hurry and I realized then I was being kidnapped—literally kidnapped.

He went speeding fast, fast, fast, and I kept trying to leap out of the car because I knew that I was in jeopardy, but he never slowed down enough for me to leave the car. When we got out to Santa Fe Springs he slowed down once near a major street crossing and I thought maybe I could escape. I actually tried to escape and he took me back into the car. He drove to a field—I guess now it's a subdivision, but in those days it was a farm and some small grain had been harvested there, maybe wheat, there was a little bit of an irrigation canal—he drove out in that field and the three of them beat me horribly.

I very nearly died from it. They took my jewelry. I had some expensive, quite valuable northern New Mexico jewelry. He took my wallet and ID, took absolutely everything I had. I was beaten so badly I was bloody with gashes, my eye was out of the socket. I crawled through the irrigation canal in mud and went up to a little road, like a country lane—now it is a major shopping center, but at the time it was in the country. I stood at the side of the road, clothing torn and blood draining from my head, and tried to signal cars.

Everybody naturally passed me by. A young man came along, very bright, alert, wonderful young man, in a terribly expensive new car, it had that new car smell. He said, "You're in trouble." I said that I had been robbed, kidnapped and beaten. He said he didn't have time to get to Los Angeles, but he knew where the Sheriff's substation was in Santa Fe Springs, so he took me to there. I went inside and I thought I would go to the washroom to check to see how badly damaged I was and to wash the worst of the blood away. I rinsed my shirt to get the worst of the blood off and I put it back on.

When I came out and went to the desk—now you have to take my word for this because I'm a fiercely truthful person—the sheriff's deputy said, recognizing me, "Mr. Kight, have you ever been arrested for morals charges before?" I said, "Listen, here I am obviously in terrible jeopardy, I've been terribly beaten, I could easily die, and you are asking about morals charges. Why aren't you asking if I need medical care? Why aren't you calling an ambulance? Why aren't you sending me to a hospital?" He said, "Well, we don't want to deal with you." I said, "I know you don't, but I need to get home. I don't have a dime to my name. I don't have any money for a cab, bus. I haven't any money to even call."

Another deputy came to stand alongside him—there were human beings even in the sheriff's department—and he said, "Mr. Kight, we'll arrange to drive you to Los Angeles city limits where we'll arrange for the next LAPD car to meet us." So the next time they went out on call, I rode with them to the city line in Los Angeles and they radioed the LAPD.

The next LAPD car that came took me in the car and they asked, "Where do you want to go?" I said, "I want to go to my car." They said, "Well, how will you get your car started, you were robbed?" I said, "I happen to have a set of keys hidden under the car." So I went to my car and managed to get back to my home at 341 South Hope Street, where I also had a key to the front door hidden. Then I got inside and by that time the swelling had begun to occur and my head was swelling. I thought if I could just get to bed (I guess by now it was 4 or 5 a.m., maybe 6) it will heal.

I woke up later in the afternoon and knew that I was in terrible trouble and I went to California Hospital over on South Hope Street, where a group of really fine doctors conducted x-rays and said, "You may not make it." After I got out of California Hospital, I went back down to 6th and Hope Street and here was that same car. I realized they were inside the bar doing the same trip. I really gave a lot of thought about how to handle that—to call the police and have them arrested. Well, what would happen? That's not my style anyway. Thrifty Drug was across the street at 6th and Hope Street. I gave a lot of thought to going over to Thrifty Drug and buying an icepick and puncturing their four tires. I stood there on 6th Street for an hour thinking about what to do. I decided not to do any of that because where I lived was isolated on the side of a hill, my house totally concealed, and they could come into my house and kill me.

During that time I was living alone. For reasons I can't possibly explain, my male–male companionships have also been sometimes of five years duration—five years and then breakup, five years and then breakup. Maybe that was just as well, because some companions I had during that time really complained a lot about how dangerous and unexpected it all was. Good grief, good grief, it was like living in a prison cell. You're dealing with someone terribly confused, you're dealing with suicidal people. They would say, "I can't stay with all this craziness. Morris, I love you, but I'm going." So it was really hard to hold onto a companion because of the risk factor.

Then in 1967, I had an even closer call. I was on an antiwar picket line over at Coronado and Wilshire. I was engaging in an antiwar demonstration against Alcoa Corporation. When I left there I was in the mood to go to a gay bar and so I went to the Paper Doll on West 7th Street, on 7th and Westlake. Some people believed it may have been the oldest gay bar licensed in California.

It was a very old gay bar. I went there where I knew everybody and they all knew me—I had gotten a lot of them out of jail or counseled them or gotten them jobs—I was really kind of at home. There was a young man there who I found very attractive, so I came on to him and he came

on to me and we went home together back to my house. I fully expected
to make love with him, of course, and as we went along he discovered that
I was involved in the antiwar movement, and obviously being in a gay bar
he knew I was gay or could make a guess that I was. It turns out that he
had only just recently returned from Vietnam and I guess he still had all
of that anti-Asian, pro-American muddled thinking going on. We were
sitting at my table and were talking about all of that. We were talking
about the antiwar movement and Vietnam, and he leapt across the table
with a switchblade knife and stabbed me in the abdomen.

I realized I was in bad trouble. I felt that if I called an ambulance that
he would finish killing me, so I rushed out to my car and drove to the City
of Los Angeles Receiving Hospital at the corner of 6th and Union, a really
well-run, first-class emergency hospital years later—they took Senator
Robert Kennedy there the night he was shot—really first-class hospital. I
came in and they put me on a gurney and doctors were shaking their heads
and asked what happened. I said, "Well, I've lost a lot of blood." I wasn't
really conscious enough to go into detail. They said, "We'll send you to
the hospital. Where do you want to go?" I would have gone to Good
Samaritan, but I wasn't rational enough to function, so they just made the
decision for me and took me to General Hospital, where I was red
blanketed—you put a red blanket on people who are in crisis or near death.
They sent me up to emergency surgery and four doctors operated on me.
The following day when I got conscious some of the doctors came to see
me. They knew me from my antiwar work and since I was on television
quite a lot, I was really quite well known. They said, "What happened?"
So I told the truth. They said, "You could have been killed."

Question: You worked with and counseled large numbers of people.
What happened to your judgment that night? I mean you had no sense
what this guy was going to pull on you?

Morris: I've given a lot of thought to that. None of us are instant
measurers of human character. No one is so clever or alert or wise or
sophisticated as to measure all human character. So he passed the quick-
and-hasty test. He was quite well groomed, quite clean, quite polite, very
good looking, polite and eager, at least willing. He passed all the tests for
a suitable companion for the evening, except that I didn't realize that he
had had a shattering experience in Vietnam. I don't know what that was
because we didn't talk about it very much. He had killed people. He had
recently had a series of negative traumatic experiences and he wanted to
work out his revenge on somebody and I was there, and so I damn near
died.

That's really a serious question that you're asking, and answering it is probably the number one answer in the whole world—who do you trust? Who do you become companions with? Who do you make friends of? What are the criteria for that? If you have made a friend, what are the lasting components of the friendship? I think that what I'm saying is that there is some hazard in all life. However well ordered your life may be, there is some hazard. My hazard is that I damn near got killed by a homicidal maniac.

I was helping and serving people, although not for a fee, on a hands-on, one-to-one basis and enjoying doing that. I recognized there were a lot of hazards in that and I could be killed, I could be jailed, I could be arrested for conspiracy, a lot of things. I was of a mind, I was of a vision that that could happen. I have been a Gandhian pacifist for a very long time. The war arose in Indochina and—as opposed as I am to war and to violence and killing—that one seemed more evident than all others to be just the worst of wars, the worst enemy, the worst choice, just the worst. So in the very early '60s, as that war escalated, I commenced to protest it.

Segue to 1959—nine people, myself, and eight others from the War Resisters League and other organizations, went to visit with Senator John Fitzgerald Kennedy. We visited with him in his office in the Senate Office Building in Washington, DC, to remonstrate with him about his vigorous financial and moral support of the Green Berets and the rising war in Indochina. So we talked for a little while about how we wished he wouldn't do that, and he said, "You see, I gather from your accents that none of you live in Massachusetts. None of you are from my state. None of you are constituents of mine, is that correct? You're from California or New York?" We said, "Yes, we're from California and New York." He said, "Well, I guessed that. You see the voters of Massachusetts disagree with you." He whipped out six letters from the desk drawer, six letters from Massachusetts saying "right on." He said, "So you see, the voters of my state don't agree with you and I thank you for coming and you'll be shown out." I was protesting from then on.

As the war rose, I gave more and more time and energy into protesting and less and less time to serving lesbian and gay people, and I felt horrible about that. So I tried to balance it off by working more in the night. I would do the counseling or homework or whatever. I was trying to find a balance. As the war rose faster and faster and it became more and more a challenge and more and more dangerous, I founded the Dow Action Committee, the first ever antiwar group that anyone knows of, to call attention to the produce of a particular company, in this case Dow Chemical Company of Midland, Michigan. Because I knew lots of lesbian and gay people, I invited them to join me on the Dow Action Committee, which was made up of members of the Socialist Workers Party, the Socialist Party, the War Resisters League, the Peace Action Council, and other elements who came into it because they liked the idea.

But there were more independents and a number of lesbian and gay people came into the Dow Action Committee. Many didn't. Many thought that I was subversive and unpatriotic and that Morris was a communist, and I was red-baited by gay people constantly. The Committee grew faster and faster. We were the darlings of the media. The gay and lesbian people in the group, seeing how to leaflet, how to organize, how to manipulate the press, how to deal with the police, how to do a sit-in, how to do a civil disobedience, how to do a demonstration and so on, liked that. As the numbers of them rose, the nongay people left the Dow Action Committee because quite a number of them said it was being dominated by "those people," by "those kinds of people"—meaning, of course, gay.

In 1969, there were major antiwar demonstration marches in New York and San Francisco simultaneously, and I was invited as a gay person, to be one of the speakers in San Francisco. I was really honored because there were only fifteen speakers. I was introduced as a gay person. When I got upon the platform—which was three stories tall with a band, the Grateful Dead, maybe or Jefferson Airplane—Rev. Cecil Williams was one of the speakers, Dalton Trumbo was a speaker. I knew some of the speakers, we had a wonderful time, lots of camaraderie.

At some point I went to the edge of the platform and I said, "I believe there are a great many veterans of the war in Indochina out here. I would gather that you're not proud of your medals. If you're not proud of your medals, we will mail them for you to the Pentagon." And the medals rained down on the platform. It was like snow. 350,000 people were out in the Polo Grounds, bright, alert, teeth clean, see their dentist twice a year, have regular medical check-ups, shower once or twice a day, well groomed. I thought "Good grief, if these 350,000 people can't stop the war, who am I." I had what Southern Protestants called a "presentment," a magical transformation. I know this is risky language, but let me say it because I feel it. I had a "presentment." My head was spinning. I felt euphoria, I felt dizziness, I felt almost like falling, I felt "good grief, I should go home." Home to LA? No, oh no, much larger, home to lesbian/gay.

Segue to the spring of 1926. My mother, a very strange woman (I had a brother, now dead, and a sister, now dead; there were three children), she was a strange women in that she had many sides to her personality. She said, (I remember the phrase she used) she said, "Now children, today we're going to have a picnic." Very unusual because she was such a hard-working woman, but she got that levity. She had a basket of food, she said, "We're going to have lunch with your father." So my mother, my brother, my sister and I went traipsing up across our farm to a field on the back side. When we got to the edge of the field, my father was plowing with a single horse and a plow and singing an old Protestant song "I'm Going Home," in that case, meaning "I'm going home to Jesus."

He was a pretty good singer and so the four of us stood behind the field in the greenery, hearing my father sing. Sitting on that platform on October 15, 1969, I started hearing my father sing "I'm Going Home." I thought I would leave here and leave the antiwar movement, I'll remain a pacifist. I leave the antiwar movement and go home to Los Angeles and home to my people. I dislike the possessive phrase "my people" and I don't use it, so "go home." I left the platform as soon as I spoke because I was exhausted.

I received a standing ovation and I left the platform and I went down the steps and out through the tunnel to the N-Judah line, a famous railroad car in San Francisco, and rode downtown to the airline terminal, went to the airport—$12 it cost in those days to fly PSA—came home and resigned from commissions, the Peace Action Council, by telegram and letter and telephone. I resigned. The following day I announced the founding meeting of what was to become the Gay Liberation Front in LA and a meeting was held.

At the headquarters of the Homosexual Information Center over on Cahuenga West up in Cahuenga Pass, eighteen people came, mostly men, I believe all white. Ian Papp came from the Dow Action Committee. The question always was, "Morris, what is radical, what does that mean?" So we talked about that. We're going to be radical, we're going to the root cause, and before the day was out we had named ourselves the Gay Liberation Front and had settled that we would go into radical activities. We commenced to talk about radical and that day we agreed to move on Barney's Beanery because of their "Faggots stay out" sign.

The Gay Liberation Front was in five cities the first year: New York, Berkeley, Los Angeles, San Francisco, San Jose in that order. Then in 1970, 385 sprung up. It was the quickest, fastest growing nonviolent movement in history. The one in Los Angeles was different than all the others in that the one in Los Angeles, at its founding meeting, heard me talk about services, service, one-to-one, nonjudgmental, nonthreatening, nonexclusionary—those words really mean something. They're the heart and soul of the magic of the Gay and Lesbian Community Services Center which was the end result.

They heard me talk about social services. I said, "We must find some kind of energy for that." We grew, and in March of 1970, Dr. Don Kilhefner came aboard and he heard what we were doing. He thought the social service component was the most pleasing one. He wrote a six page position paper talking about systematizing the services and we got that approved by the membership. Then he said to me, "Now, we must sit for a day or two or three, or whatever it takes to get out of your head and on to paper what it is you've been doing, because nobody knows all of that or where all that came from."

You see I had not kept records for many years. The police raided my home a number of times and they were always interested in address lists and correspondence and so on, so I learned to burn that as quickly as it had been acted upon. So I had no papers of any kind. It was all in the head, it was all oral. I sat with Don for three days and got out of my head and on to paper, psychiatry, social worker, probation, courts, judges, police, bail bondspersons, jobs, employers, how to deal with an employer, how to be honest and still get the job, and so on. That became the Gay Survival Committee of the Gay Liberation Front. I liked that a lot so I gave about half attention to the Gay Survival Committee and one-quarter attention to demonstrating in the streets, and one-quarter attention to the antiwar movement because the war in Indochina was still going on.

The Gay Survival Committee grew and grew and grew and became more attractive. More people came into it as volunteers and there was in-house training, and retraining, and counterculture activities, music, art, theater, and so on. All that grew while the Gay Liberation Front died off because it had fulfilled its basic purpose. Its basic purpose was to therapize lesbian and gay persons of any feelings of alleged inferiority. We had been our own worst enemy. We had believed in our sickness, our sinfulness. We had really believed that. But now there was the beginning of what would eventually become the world's first and largest gay and lesbian social services center.

After one of the quickest nonviolent social revolutions in history, from 1969 to 1971, a number of highly successful and still ongoing institutions were created: the annual celebration of lesbian/gay pride, Christopher Street West, of which I was the principal founder on May 12 1970; and the Gay and Lesbian Community Services Center which I, Don Kilhefner, and other socially concerned citizens created. Each year on the last Sunday of June, when I go down Santa Monica Boulevard in West Hollywood, I am unbelievably enchanted, and the days when I walk down Hudson Avenue in Hollywood where the Center is now located, I have to choke back the tears. Tears of joy and of pride, and of how far we have all come.

Chapter 3

Gay men and psychiatry

A professional and personal account

In the 1970s, a 30 year old architect, who had had exclusive homosexual fantasies since early life and had never experienced pleasurable heterosexual sex, decided to enter psychoanalytic therapy with a well-trained, well-thought-of psychiatrist and psychoanalyst. He asked: "Tell me Doctor, if at the end of this therapy I wind up as a homosexual, will you consider this treatment a failure?" As an experienced therapist, the psychiatrist replied in the usual professional way: "Why do you ask? How would you feel about it?" The patient persisted and said: "No, I want an answer. If you won't answer I will have to leave the treatment." The doctor answered: "Well, that is a difficult question and I will answer it, but I will need some time to think it over."

At the next appointment, the patient asked if the doctor had his response. The psychiatrist responded: "I've given this a great deal of thought and I have to tell you, yes, I would consider it a failure." The patient said: "I appreciate your honesty but I will find a psychiatrist who doesn't have this prejudice." Unfortunately, most gay men in the 1940s, 1950s, and 1960s did not ask that question.

Typical of the era before gay liberation are the following cases of patients who were brought to a psychiatric clinic in the 1950s (see Sanders, 1980):

1 A 17 year old boy who was brought by his parents after they came home early one night and walked in on their son having sex with a male friend.
2 Several men, some of whom were married, who came to the clinic in an acute anxiety state after being arrested in a public toilet or in a park and were sent by a judge as a condition of probation.
3 A man in his mid-50s who came with his wife, after he announced that he wanted to leave her and their three children. He gave a history of increasing impotence and expressed fears of homosexuality. On

detailed inquiry it turned out that he had had fleeting homosexual thoughts of about six months' duration.

4   A man in his early 30s who wanted to change his sexual orientation after having lived as a practicing homosexual for the last ten years. He had never been able to have a sustained relationship and had only been able to have homosexual relationships after he had several alcoholic drinks.

5   A man in his early 30s who had been passed over for a promotion when his employers found out that he was a homosexual.

6   A 40 year old man who, living with a homosexual lover, was experiencing impotence or sometimes premature ejaculations.

While homosexuality was an issue in all of these cases, in most, it was the least important. However, teachers and supervisors in psychiatric residency and medical schools, with a few notable exceptions, viewed these men as experiencing specific problems about homosexuality itself. Yet, of those who came for treatment and mentioned homosexuality as part of their lives, some functioned in the world competently and productively; others performed poorly. Sometimes they were in crisis, sometimes not. Some were intelligent; some were not. Some were psychotic or neurotic; and others had severe personality disorders. Many faced overwhelming problems. They often came with experiences of family or social rejection, and occasionally both. They were at different stages in the life cycle and they had all the developmental crises that are suggestive of each life stage. They were also at different stages in their self-acceptance as homosexuals or their coming out.

Like most people growing up during the 1950s, they incorporated society's stereotypical and negative views of homosexuality. It was quite surprising, then, that they often had a healthy amount of self-esteem and many psychological strengths. But what was even more surprising was that the professionals failed to see this and proceeded to focus on the pathology of homosexuality as if the homosexuality was the most important part of the total personality.

HOMOSEXUALITY AS MENTAL ILLNESS

Until the 1970s, the general consensus in the psychiatric and psychological professions was that homosexuality, in and of itself, was a reflection of mental illness. This was repeatedly propounded in the professional literature as well as in the popular culture of Western society. The professional climate could be compared to living in the times of Galileo, when most of the population thought that the earth was flat and the sun rotated about the earth. Although some thought the earth was indeed round and rotated around the sun, most scientists and the public believed that if you sailed off far enough into *Terra Incognita* you would fall off.

The majority of psychiatrists, psychologists, and other psychotherapists in practice during the better part of the twentieth century have similarly held erroneous beliefs, in this case, that homosexuality is an illness. They perceived it as an illness that, acquired by social experience, could be cured by a good interpersonal therapeutic experience. They defined it as a chosen way of life (a "lifestyle") that was incompatible with the perceived typical, normal, healthy, happy heterosexual life.

However, at that time, these views were thought to be liberal and enlightened, as opposed to a reactionary view of homosexual behavior as moral degradation or sin. There have been, and continue to be, many distortions, myths, stereotypes, and prejudices about gay and lesbian people. The most common include the supposition that gays are immoral and promiscuous, want to be the opposite sex, hate the opposite sex, are interested in sex with children, recruit young people into a homosexual life, are effeminate (gay men) or butch (lesbians), have severe psychopathology, and have a lonely old age. The professionals who treated homosexuals knew little of gay life and the social world of these men and women. Basically, they viewed homosexuality as incompatible with a reasonably happy, productive life. One source of their information was psychiatric textbooks.

A review of some psychiatric textbooks published in the 1940s, 1950s, and 1960s, reveals several common themes about homosexuality, including:

1 The etiology of homosexuality is unclear.
2 There is a possible constitutional cause.
3 Oedipal complexes, fear of women, seductive mothers, distant fathers, and related psychoanalytic theories are relevant to consider.
4 Treatments are possible, but the results are unclear.

Confusion about the subject is evident from these texts. The only other major source of information about homosexuals for psychiatrists was acquired from their patients—hardly a representative group. Rarely did they think their relatives, colleagues, or friends might be gay or lesbian. Gay men were essentially invisible to most professionals other than as patients, and lesbians were even more so. Many lesbians then, as now, were often reluctant to see a male psychotherapist, and in an era when most therapists were men, lesbians remained hidden. One need only look at the psychological and psychiatric literature about homosexuality prior to the 1970s to confirm the absence of information on lesbians.

Female sexuality was never taken as seriously as male sexuality by the psychiatric and psychological communities. Only in the relatively recent past has there been a wholesale revision in Freudian theory about female sexuality. Surprisingly, even many women psychoanalysts rarely questioned established thought about such subjects as "penis envy," let alone homosexuality. A few case reports and an article by Freud were about all there was on the topic of women's sexuality. Yet, several prominent orthodox psychoanalysts were known to be lesbians. This seemed not to affect their male colleagues, since it was a topic never discussed. By and large, they were held in high regard, achieving positions of influence and power within the psychoanalytic institutes and various university departments of psychiatry.

Part of the invisibility was due to society's perception about unmarried women. No one thought very much about an unmarried woman living alone or two women sharing an apartment or a house together. Most people thought of the women as "unlucky," that is, unable to find a man to marry, or as spinsters who cared for their aging parents. The so-called "Boston marriage" of two women sharing a house together was a part of the American social scene.

On the other hand, professional men who were known or thought to be homosexual were treated with suspicion. Very few, if any, would have been admitted to a psychoanalytic institute. The few who were had to have their psychoanalysts collude with them in keeping it a secret. They could practice only by being in the closet. If these closeted professionals were the only role models, it is not surprising that younger gay professionals, while in training, felt they were carrying a bad secret and, on some level, reinforcing society's homophobic attitudes.

"CURING" HOMOSEXUALITY

In the mid-1950s homosexuality was listed in the *Diagnostic and Statistical Manual of Mental Disorders* of the American Psychiatric Association under the general heading of the sociopathic disorders, lumping it together with antisocial and criminal behavior. As a result, treatment included every method used by psychiatrists in managing problems of mental illnesses, such as electro-shock treatment, lobotomy, aversion therapy, castration, hormone therapy, formal psychoanalysis, psychoanalytic psychotherapy, and group therapies of various types. Some of these treatments worked temporarily, but so does torture.

Some change-oriented therapists encouraged change openly, defining heterosexual performance as the only way to a mentally healthy life. Others, more subtly, analyzed everything related to homosexual thoughts or feelings of the patient as bad or neurotic or sick, and everything related to heterosexuality as good and healthy.

Some of the more influential approaches to change-oriented therapy included Kolb and Johnson (1955: 507), who described the precipitating factors that led to the overt eruption of homosexual behavior as "the unconscious permissiveness of one parent with the other parent more or less condoning. ... It is suggested that overt homosexuality, as well as other aberrant behavior, may be induced or persist through the technique employed by a therapist." They suggested that the therapist, once he had a grasp of the psychodynamics of the case, prohibit the expression of homosexual behavior and interrupt treatment if the homosexual behavior was resumed "until the patient is willing to give up the behavior and face the consequent frustration anxiety and rage that then ensues" (Kolb and Johnson, 1955: 507–8).

Ovesey (1965) pointed out that those persons who are exclusively homosexual are phobic of women, and of the genitals in particular, and suggested that while analysis of the phobias was important, this phobia, like others, is only resolved by the patient's facing the phobic situation. He further suggested (1965: 222) that the only way individuals will ultimately resolve these fears is "in bed with a woman" repeatedly until potency and pleasure are achieved.

Bieber *et al.* (1962: 265) listed the following reasons that homosexuals are resistant to treatment, and said that these reasons constitute the core fear complex around which a defensive structure of denial and resistance is organized:

1 Unconscious fear of discovering heterosexual wishes and feelings.
2 Greater fear of acting on them.
3 Fear of discovering the inevitable emotional bankruptcy of homosexuality.
4 Fear of an inability to shift to heterosexuality.

Anna Freud (1949: 195) noted that in her experience men "turn towards the other sex when they realize the 'strong man' whom they chose as partner represents their own lost masculinity."

In short, these and other professionals (including Bergler, 1951; Hadden, 1966; Hatterer, 1970; and Socarides, 1968), although not being able to document a sustained change in sexual orientation, strongly believed that treatment of the psychoneurotic problems of gay men should focus on altering their orientation in the direction of heterosexuality. They spoke at meetings, wrote papers, and widely espoused their views. They were frequently quoted and referred to in the literature and in textbooks. Their perspectives formed the dominant conceptualizations about homosexuality in the 1950s and 1960s, despite some growing evidence to the contrary (such as Hooker, 1957).

These value-laden, sometimes obscurantist, approaches to therapy had the approval of most mental health professionals. Although Freud said in his letter to an American mother that "Homosexuality is assuredly no advantage but it is nothing to be ashamed of, no vice, no degradation. It cannot be classified as an illness: We consider it to be a variation of the sexual functions produced by a certain arrest of sexual development," homosexuality was widely considered to be *prima facie* evidence of mental illness or at the very least unresolved oedipal difficulties and castration fears.

DEPATHOLOGIZING HOMOSEXUALITY

However, criticisms of the dominant perspectives grew, especially in the years following the Stonewall rebellion. The treatment strategies and theoretical positions of change-oriented psychiatrists and psychologists were starting to be viewed as based, in most part, upon society's antihomosexual prejudices and stereotypes. They were seen as oversimplified: they overlooked and discounted the complexity of the etiological factors that cause sexuality and the impossibility of an individual making a change in sexual orientation, even though it wasn't for lack of trying different techniques. Furthermore, the problem of these approaches was that they each viewed homosexuality in different ways.

Underlying these forms of treatment were certain assumptions, values, and methods of framing the problem that obscured an appropriate therapeutic approach to the homosexual. First, the term "homosexual" was applied to a wide range of behavior, from the single adolescent episode of homosexual behavior to a long-term pattern of homosexual sexual and social life. Often those involved in these very different kinds of behavior were described, in a universal sweep, as homosexuals.

Second, there was a tendency toward generalization, that is, the notion that all persons who exhibit homosexual behavior fall into a single group. Schizophrenic, sociopathic, child-molesting individuals, along with the competent functioning individuals, were all lumped together into one category. Instead of exploring the diverse aspects of their personality functioning, therapists and researchers discussing homosexuality focused primarily, sometimes exclusively, on the communality of their homosexual behavior.

Third, many therapists focused on the homosexual orientation and behavior of a patient as if that behavior caused whatever personality difficulties the patient presented. Thus, homosexual behavior was seen as the cause of depression, anxiety, psychosis, personality disorder, or the patient's being stuck at a particular stage of psychosexual development (whatever that meant). All aspects of personality were viewed through the screen of "deviant" sexuality.

Fourth, most studies of homosexual men were studies of patients, that is, men who sought psychological help. What the patients told the therapist about the problems of homosexuality was assumed to be true of nonpatient homosexuals as well.

Fifth, societal prejudice against homosexual behavior was strong, hence therapeutic practices often seemed less designed to help the patient than to enforce the values of the therapist on the patient.

Although Evelyn Hooker's (1957) research had challenged quite strongly the assumptions and findings of the dominant theories, it wasn't until fifteen years later that some eminent psychiatrists, such as Judd Marmor, actively attempted to change the profession's official views. In December 1973, the American Psychiatric Association finally deleted homosexuality from the second edition of the *Diagnostic and Statistical Manual for Mental Disorders (DSM-II)*. The American Psychological Association similarly reaffirmed the depathologizing of homosexuality in a resolution in 1974. And in 1988, the ambiguous diagnosis "ego-dystonic homosexuality," which had remained in the DSM, was removed. Homosexual behavior itself was no longer *ipso facto* a sign of mental disorder. This change occurred not without considerable debate and difference of opinion within the mental health professions.

There were reports in the literature (such as Bieber *et al.*, 1962; Hadden, 1966) that suggested that aversive therapy for some highly motivated individuals had been able to suppress homosexual feelings, urges, and behaviors and permit the development and practice of heterosexual behaviors. These reports omitted any detailed dynamic descriptions of the subjects and any followup data, while claiming varying degrees of success (Davison, 1991). Yet, years of research and reviews of studies have failed to sustain these early claims. As the opening statement from the American Psychological Association's "Fact Sheet on Reparative Therapy" phrases it: "No scientific evidence exists to support the effectiveness of any of the conversion therapies that try to change sexual orientation" (quoted in Haldeman, 1991). It is this view that dominates today's psychiatric and psychological professions.

DAVID SANDERS: A PERSONAL PERSPECTIVE

When I decided to apply for a psychiatric residency in 1956, the mental illness model of homosexuality was dominant. My motivation to become a psychiatrist was mixed. On one hand, I wanted to be trained as a psychiatrist as a result of seeing the psychological problems in my pediatric practice and the problems connected with the public health aspects of my work as Director of the Cerebral Palsy Program of the New York City Department of Health. On the other hand, I thought that this would be a good way for me to get into psychoanalytic treatment, without the stigma of being labeled "a patient." In the 1950s, there was a stigma attached to seeing a therapist, but it was accepted if you were in treatment as a requirement of a training program.

At that time, I had identified myself as having homosexual desires and had participated in many homosexual experiences since adolescence. By the age of 19, I thought of myself as a homosexual man. This was not without inner turmoil. I had not, however, come out in my professional life or with my heterosexual friends and family.

In the mid-1950s, I was troubled about the direction my life was taking. I was 29 and experiencing the difficulty in establishing a permanent relationship that many homosexual men have. Having grown up in a close family where divorce was unthinkable, I thought that the only way to live was in a permanent, preferably monogamous, relationship. Today, I see the problems of that time in a somewhat different light, more as a "coming out" problem, more as problems in dealing with my having internalized society's homophobia.

But during the 1940s and 1950s, many gay men entered therapy, rather than viewing their problems as issues related to society's negative, stereotyped perspectives. A number of discussions by gay men of their analysis point out in detail the problems faced in treatment during that period. Two in particular come to mind: noted public health physician Howard Brown's (1976) *Familiar Faces, Hidden Lives* and historian Martin Duberman's (1991) *Cures*. Both men describe horrendous therapeutic experiences with attempted "reparative" therapies. The problems they wrote about, similar to ones I will describe, were problems of psychiatrists being unable to conceive of homosexuality as a variation of sexual functioning that could be positive. It would be easy to say that their personal psychopathology made them remain in treatments of the type they describe, but in fact their treatment was approved and recommended by the culture of the era.

For example, I have interviewed in my practice more that twenty men who confirm similar sexual orientation change treatments during that period of psychological thought. One patient told me about his treatment with a famous psychoanalyst who said to him on his second visit, "If you come into treatment with me, we'll have none of this adjustment crap. You are here to become heterosexual."

Meanwhile, I was accepted for a psychiatric residency in 1956 at the Presbyterian Hospital–New York Psychiatric Institute program of Columbia University and assigned to the children's service. I had been trained as a practicing pediatrician, and because of this I felt comfortable with the assignment. There were nine members of the first-year residency class, a fairly tight knit group, and soon most of us became friends. I thought one of the other residents in the group might be gay, which turned out to be the case.

Within three months, all but one of the residents started in psychoanalytic treatment. At that time, while it was not required that all psychiatric residents enter treatment, it was strongly encouraged by all our teachers as well as the more senior residents. I promptly began a series of consultations to start psychoanalysis.

I began analysis with one of the senior teachers in the department, a highly respected woman. During the consultations she seemed warm and caring and eager to help me. When I entered treatment, I was having a somewhat troubled relationship with a man. Very early in the analysis, it became clear, however, that the goal of the therapist's treatment was to change my sexual orientation, rather than to deal with the troubling relationship. Anything that had to do with homosexuality was defined as disturbed and pathological. Everything that had to do with my friendliness or liking for women was defined as healthy and positive.

As I proceeded to recount the story of my life, my mother was described as being overly controlling and my father as too passive. My relations with my parents were skillfully woven, slowly and carefully, and with utmost clinical skill, into a dynamic picture which began to account for my homosexuality. I, eagerly and rationally (or so I thought then), was a partner in these formulations. My associations and dreams seemed to fit these assumptions perfectly. Instead of being a homosexual, I was slowly defined and defining myself as a latent heterosexual.

Now, as I write this, it sounds as if I were the passive participant in this four-times-a-week process. But this was not so. Once I caught on to the way things were being formulated, I joined in enthusiastically. I was encouraged by this definition of myself as a latent heterosexual and felt relieved by the overt as well as the subtle suggestions that a "cure" was both possible as well as desirable.

The psychoanalyst made passing reference to other patients she had treated who were not very different from me, who had married and had children. At one point she alluded to a collection of photos that these patients had sent her of their children, her "homosexual grandchildren" as she referred to them. I broke up with my lover of a year or so, feeling both relieved and sad. I saw the world in front of me as being open to both professional and social success, the social success of course being happily and contentedly heterosexual.

When tension began to rise in me, I was told that this was to be expected as sexual problems were notoriously difficult, but with hard work on both our parts, success could be achieved. Homosexual sexual abstinence was also explicitly suggested and encouraged. Freud's views on abstinence as a way of provoking the psyche to bring up pertinent and important material in dreams and associations, as well as a way to hurry treatment along, were used as the model.

In addition, the therapist strongly recommended that I start dating women. The notion was put forward that I was phobic of women because of my relationship with my mother and that the way to get over this was to have more contact with them. It was also suggested that as I had more contact with women I would become more sexually aroused by them in a healthy way, and my latent heterosexuality would come forth.

Heterosexual abstinence, however, was not prescribed. In fact, just the reverse: every heterosexual response was strongly encouraged. It seems in retrospect, over thirty-five years later, that my sexual orientation was worked on as if it were a totally learned response, as a reflection of my relationship with my close binding mother and my distant father. The fact that my father was shy and reserved but not distant, rarely got talked about.

Being a "good boy," a cooperative patient, and a hard-working student, I accepted all of this without question. I started dating a very nice young woman and, indeed, had sex with her. But, it never felt the same. I did it like it was homework. Nothing, of course, was ever spoken about the effect a relationship with a basically homosexual man might have on a woman. This woman psychoanalyst seemed to have little regard for anyone but her patients' welfare, that is, her interpretation of what her patients' welfare was.

Unfortunately, my therapist's views were also those of my residency supervisors and other teachers. Nowhere in the training program was the topic of the evaluation and treatment of the homosexual patient discussed in an organized and accurate fashion. It was only mentioned in the context of how to manage, approach, and try to help the individual patient. The helping, however, always included an attempt at changing the patient's sexual orientation, even if he did not desire such a change.

Many of the clinicians wanted to do psychotherapeutic work with their homosexual patients, but thought that a focus on the sexuality was essential to do that work. As a result, I found myself treating my patients as I was being treated and as I was taught. This caused needless stress to the patients and me. When I finished my residency, I made it a point not to take homosexual men as patients. For several years, I avoided the issue until the profession started rethinking its positions and I became more open about my own homosexuality.

Until then, I continued to have relationships with women, but they never felt as though this was really what I desired. My fantasies remained about men. Yet I remained in analysis for four years. There were many other issues dealt with in the course of the psychoanalysis; many aspects of my personality and functioning were clarified and I did make many significant changes that were positive and helpful.

However, the analyst was unwilling to continue treatment if I "reverted" to a homosexual life. After much internal debate and discussion with the therapist, I decided to interrupt for a while. I began to feel much better and to see my homosexual friends. I started to have homosexual experiences and relationships again. My work continued successfully and I was functioning more positively in all ways. It was as if a great burden—trying to be someone other than myself—had been lifted from me. About six months later, in 1962, I met a man whom I thought I could be happy with. I went back to see the analyst to discuss it. She said that she was not interested in continuing treatment with me if I continued the relationship with this man. More than thirty years later we are still together. I have never regretted the choice.

Chapter 4

Interview with Judd Marmor, M.D.

Question: What was it like treating gay men in the 1940s and how has it changed over time?

Marmor: Let me see if I can describe the psychoanalytic view of homosexuality at that time. I was trained at the New York Psychoanalytic Institute, which was a classically oriented institute. Everything was taught according to strictly Freudian concepts. However, my own analyst, Abram Kardiner, was one of the early ego psychologists in psychoanalysis who was beginning to question the libido theory. I went to him because I knew that. Even as a psychiatric resident, knowing I wanted to get psychoanalytic training (in the 1930s that was the only way to get some understanding of psychotherapeutic process), I found certain of Freud's formulations a little difficult to swallow, and I was looking for somebody who would have an open mind towards changing concepts.

The attitude toward homosexuality in those days was similar in all the psychoanalytic institutes. There was supposed to be a uniform "homosexual personality." That personality was considered to be emotionally immature and incapable of forming meaningful "object relationships." I remember going to a meeting about homosexuality at one of the psychoanalytic society programs, and all of the presentations dealt with how "vindictive, intolerant, sadomasochistic, incapable of love" and so on all homosexuals were. That just didn't make sense to me, even then, as a young psychiatrist.

This was around 1940 or 1941. I got out of medical school in 1933. I began my psychoanalytic training in 1937 at the New York Psychoanalytic Institute. This meeting was either in the late '30s or early '40s. The prevailing assumption was that homosexuals—incidentally, the emphasis was on homosexual men, there was very little said or written about lesbians in those days—all grew up in families of unloving, distant fathers and binding, seductive mothers, and that they developed an incestuous attachment to the mother with resultant castration anxiety that prevented them from having a sexual relationship with a woman. In a paper that I presented about five years ago, I summarized my reservations concerning the classical psychoanalytic formulations of those early years.

I'll read an excerpt from that unpublished paper. I wrote then:

Research developments over the past twenty years have generated doubts concerning the validity of some traditional psychoanalytic formulations about the nature and origins of male homosexual behavior. One major reservation [this is one that I recognized very early] rests on the fact that these formulations have been based for the most part on clinical experience with homosexual patients in therapy and thus represent a skewed sampling of the total homosexual population, most of whom neither wanted nor sought therapy for their sexual preference. In addition, the intrinsic validity of some of these formulations began to be questioned.

For example, the most frequently employed explanation for male homosexual behavior is the presence of castration anxiety as formulated by Fenichel in 1945, due to incestuous guilt feelings deriving from a seductive mother and hostile or unloving father. Thus, because all women were seen as castrated persons, they aroused the castration anxiety of homosexual men and were, therefore, unconsciously feared and sexually avoided. However, castration anxiety was also used as the explanation for a wide variety of other psychiatric conditions, including most of the neuroses, as well as the entire range of the paraphilias. Actually, symbolic castration anxiety can be consistently demonstrated in most male patients, even though they do not demonstrate any overt homosexual proclivities! Moreover, if such fears are responsible for the heterosexual inhibitions of homosexual men, how can the behavior of bisexual men, many of whom find heterosexual intercourse quite pleasurable, be understood?

A number of other traditional assumptions about homosexual psychodynamics are similarly contradictory. One of these is that homosexuals are deeply narcissistic individuals, who are therefore attracted to persons like themselves. But narcissistic personalities exist in wide profusion among heterosexuals also, and this cannot, therefore, be an adequate explanation for homosexual behavior. Another common hypothesis is that male homosexuals hate or fear women because of powerful unconscious negative feelings toward their own mothers. Yet we know that many male homosexuals have close and affectionate relationships with women. A contrary postulation is that male homosexuals are strongly identified with their mothers, hence their erotic responsiveness toward men. Still another proposition asserts that obligatory homosexual behavior in men is the outcome of the pre-Oedipal problems of separation and individuation. However, similar pre-Oedipal problems of separation and individuation are demonstrable in many neurotic heterosexuals. None of these formulations, therefore, can in themselves be sufficient explanations for obligatory male homosexuality.

The simple fact is that although one or another of these dynamic patterns can indeed be demonstrated in some homosexual men, they are not present in others, and none of them is pathognomonic.

Probably the most widely held analytic assumption about the etiology of homosexual behavior is that it is specifically induced by a parental constellation of a close-binding, seductive mother and a distant, unloving father. This family background is considered to be the primary basis for the castration anxieties, the fear/hate of women, the feminine identification, etc. seen in homosexual male patients. However, other studies (such as Siegelman, 1974) have demonstrated that such parental constellations can also be found in the backgrounds of a great many heterosexual men in whom they have not led to homosexual behavior. Secondly, many homosexuals, particularly nonpatient homosexuals, have been shown to come from quite varied family backgrounds. As a matter of fact, over fifty variables in maternal, paternal, sibling family patterns have been found in male homosexuals: loving mothers, hostile mothers, loving fathers, hostile fathers, idealized fathers, sibling rivalries, broken homes, absent mothers, absent fathers, etc.

Similarly, the assumption that a truly loving father absolutely precludes the development of homosexuality in a son (that was one of Bieber's "axioms") is simply not true. I have personally known and treated a number of male homosexuals who had very warm and positive relationships with their fathers; and the comprehensive study of the development of sexual preference by Bell, Weinberg, and Hammersmith (1981) revealed that 17 percent of the male homosexual subjects felt themselves to be their father's favorite.

Another shortcoming in traditional conceptions about homosexuality was the tendency of some authors to talk of homosexuals as if they are all alike psychodynamically, i. e., "the homosexual personality." This fails to take cognizance of the wide diversity of homosexual personalities, a diversity which is just as great as that which exists for heterosexuals—from healthy normals to disturbed psychotics.

Question: As you were facing these issues at that time, how did you treat your patients, say in the 1940s and 1950s when you moved to California and became successful and began to see homosexual patients?

Marmor: In each instance I worked with them trying to see if they could begin to enjoy sex with women. In those days, most of the men I saw were willing to try. They were deeply influenced by the prevailing cultural attitudes and they felt homophobically rejecting of their own sexual patterns. A number of them did succeed in having heterosexual intercourse, but it was clear to me and to them that it just wasn't what they really wanted. As my work with them progressed I focused instead on trying to help them accept themselves and achieve a meaningful bonding in a homosexual relationship.

Then, in the early 1960s, Arthur Rosenthal, the editor of Basic Books, contacted me and said, "I'd like you to do a book for us; what would you like to do it on? Is there anything in your analytic work that you'd like to write about?" I replied, "Well, one thing is that I believe the prevailing analytic attitudes toward homosexuality are wrong." He said, "Great, do a book on that." My reply was, "Well, I don't feel like writing a whole book on it, but I'll edit a book on it. I think homosexuality has multiple roots and I want to get a geneticist, a sociologist, a biologist, an endocrinologist, an anthropologist, an historian, etc. and have each one describe how the problem appears from their point of view." Rosenthal agreed, and that was the genesis of my first edited book on homosexuality, *Sexual Inversion: The Multiple Roots of Homosexuality* (1965).

You'll note that, in the first chapter, there's one statement that I made that indicated that I was still caught up to some degree in a traditional assumption about homosexuals:

Within the matrix of contemporary western civilization, with its abhorrence of and hostility to homosexual behavior and its powerful pressures toward heterosexual conformity, it does not seem likely that a homosexual object choice ... could maintain itself in a hostile and punitive environment, *unless there were concomitant anxieties of equal or greater strength blocking the path to heterosexual adaptation.* For our time and culture, therefore, the psychoanalytic assumption that preferential homosexual behavior is always associated with unconscious fears of heterosexual relationships appears valid.

(Marmor, 1965: 11–12, italics added)

That shows where my thinking was in 1965. Nevertheless, *Sexual Inversion* became a landmark. It broke fresh ground in the psychoanalytic literature of the time.

Question: But you wish you could erase that particular passage?

Marmor: Yes I do, and I did reject it in my later writings, because of subsequent research and my growing awareness that there were other factors involved that we psychiatrists simply were not taking into consideration. What I deal with in the paper, from which I quoted earlier, is the "psychological reductionism" of early psychoanalysis that assumed that any deviant pattern of behavior *had* to be due to early life conditioning. We ignored the genetic, the prenatal, and the hormonal factors that also entered into the pattern. It was that that led us to assume that infantile autism was the mother's fault or that schizophrenia was caused by schizophrenogenic mothers. I weep when I think of what we did to mothers, when I think of the thousands of mothers who were forced to live with guilt feelings about their autistic, schizophrenic, and homosexual children!

I also wish I could redo one serious mistake that I made in my second edited book, *Homosexual Behavior: A Modern Reappraisal* (1980). I picked the wrong man to write the history. I should have picked—what was his name?—John Boswell. He was the man I should have picked. I had nothing but trouble with Arno Karlen, the person I chose, who turned out to be a disciple of Bieber's—a fact that I had not known. I tried to edit out as much of his homophobia as I could, but some of it still crept in. I would be very proud of the book but for that flaw.

Question: But you were able to change your views. Why didn't other psychoanalysts see the light?

Marmor: You know, one tends to get brainwashed in psychoanalytic training. All the "wise elders" say that something is this way or that, and all the books are written, confirm it, and above all, Freud said it was so! My ability to move in different directions was actually helped by my 1965 book, faulty though it was. What it did was to open the doors for me to more frequent contacts with nonpatient gay men and women than I had ever had before.

I then began to see and experience the diversity of homosexual individuals at first hand. That's why the second book had to come out. But, at the same time, a lot of research was taking place involving prenatal androgenization. As a matter of fact, I'm trying to think through a potential ethical dilemma that this newer research presents. Assuming that we learn that predisposition to homosexuality may well be caused by the prenatal level of androgenization, is it possible that this may be used by people as a way of "preventing" homosexuality? It's very possible that it might! The challenge then becomes to recognize that perhaps the development of homosexuality has positive values both evolutionarily and socially. Wilson, the Harvard sociobiologist, has already made a beginning in this direction, and we may well learn that the kind of sensitivity and the perspectives that gay men and women possess enrich our society and aren't things that we should try to prevent!

Question: But maybe the sensitivities come from being oppressed, not from the androgens, and so if we no longer are oppressed, then we wouldn't be any more sensitive than anybody else.

Marmor: Perhaps. There are many unanswered questions. I can see why gay men and women might feel a little uncomfortable about this kind of research, however, and what its ultimate implications might be.

Question: What do you think the balance is between biology and environmental factors in homosexuality.

Marmor: I think that biology creates a predisposition that is very important. It is not the only factor, however, because identical twin studies indicate that there must be an environmental component also. The biological predisposition factor, nevertheless, is unquestionably important. We now know that in identical twins there's a much greater incidence of homosexuality than in fraternal twins. But it can be influenced by environmental factors. I must say that I tend to lean more and more toward predisposition as a major factor, but I do think that once a child has that predisposition, that a whole series of consequences occur in how the mother treats him, in how the father treats him, how his peer group treats him. Those things have to have some effect.

Question: But one failure of the biological research of Simon LeVay and others, is that they fail to make clear who's a homosexual. How do you genetically determine that? They often go by behavior rather than just by fantasy. There are heterosexual men who are married but who think about men when they are having sex with their wives. And what about heterosexual men in prison who engage in homosexual sex? Are their hypothalamuses different now because they engage in same-sex sex in prison?

Marmor: That's different. I don't consider that genuine homosexuality. That's situational homosexuality. Don't you think in a way it's something like being left-handed? You can force a kid to be right-handed, but they'll never feel comfortable being right-handed. That's what I'm coming to believe more and more.

Question: Did you find that as you were learning more about this in the 1940s, '50s, and '60s your treatment toward gay men changed? What did you do differently?

Marmor: I stopped interpreting that their homosexuality was something due to an unconscious fear of heterosexuality. I left the matter of attempting to have heterosexual relations up to the men themselves. As you know, many gay men are capable of having heterosexual relationships. They just don't enjoy them as much as they do homosexual ones.

I remember a young man whom I treated only about nine or ten years ago when my newer ideas were pretty solidly established. He was caught in a conflict in that he was able to have perfectly effective and satisfying sex with women, but he was strongly drawn to men. After trying heterosexuality out with a woman for almost a year—he didn't marry her, thank goodness—he said to me, "You know it just isn't the same thing. I don't get the same kick out of it with women as I do with men." I said, "Fine, then let's forget about it and focus on your relationships with men and on developing the kind of pairing that you're looking for." I have yet to meet a gay man who didn't really want to have a permanent or meaningful partner if he could. I suppose there are exceptions. There must be homosexual bachelors just as there are heterosexual bachelors, but I am convinced that most people want to solve the problem of their inner loneliness by finding a partner with whom they can share their life. This young patient of mine did go on to find such a partner, and he was much happier thereafter.

Question: So in the 1940s you would have treated him to overcome his fear of women?

Marmor: Yes, I might have pushed him harder in the direction of trying to make it work, to have children, to become part of the mainstream. I think that one of the wonderful things that our research study interviewing successful gay men has done is to demonstrate the richness and satisfaction that can exist in a homosexual life. I think that's very important for all psychiatrists and psychotherapists to know.

Question: What did patients come to you with? I mean when patients came to you in the 1940s, how did they present the problem as opposed to now? How has that changed?

Marmor: It has changed in recent years because there's a much greater self-acceptance among homosexuals. The great self-loathing that appears in *The Boys in the Band*, for example, was something that I saw commonly in the 1940s. The author of that play obviously hated being gay. Why? He was brainwashed by the culture. All the patients that I saw in the 1940s and early '50s were people who were damaged by the homophobia of our society and wanted to change their homosexuality if they possibly could. Their self-image was painfully damaged. They believed that they were inferior in one way or another. And, of course, when I encounter that now, my approach to it is very different. "It's not you," I say, "it's the society that's wrong." I give them the example of a Jew who hates being Jewish or a Catholic who hates being Catholic because of society's prejudices. The problem is in society; it's not in being Catholic, Jewish, or whatever else.

Question: How did psychoanalysts, from the 1940s and into the 1960s, think about the women that they were encouraging these gay men to get sexually involved with. That really is using these women for a kind of experimental purpose. It must have been a really terrible experience for most of them.

Marmor: Women have terrible experiences with heterosexuals, too! I guess we were on the side of our patients and wanted to help them achieve their goal if it could be achieved, and the women were merely instruments. After all, a lot of women were starting to have extramarital intercourse in those days and we were beginning to go beyond the stage where there was a moral restriction about that—at least among most of the analysts that I knew.

The real problem was that heterosexual psychoanalysts, for the most part, were simply unable to project themselves into the feelings of a male who had the same kind of natural proclivity towards the same sex that the analyst had towards the opposite sex. That's what fascinates me about Charles Socarides and his views. He has really done much damage.

In a legal case that we were both involved some fifteen years or more ago, I represented a male civilian employee who had been fired by the Navy when it was discovered that he was gay even though he was one of their best people. Socarides was called in as the Navy's expert. He described all homosexual men as being "compulsively driven" to having sex with other men. On the basis of that, he considered them so pathological that their mental status bordered on psychosis. Yet I remember when I was a young man, when I was in my late teens and early 20s, I could hardly think of anything else except finding a woman to have sex with.

What Socarides seems unable to understand is that the behavior of homosexuals is no different than that of heterosexuals of comparable ages. Look at all the sexual harassment that goes on all the time in the military on the part of heterosexuals toward women.

Question: When gay people come to you now, what are their issues? Do they still want to change, to become straight?

Marmor: No, they come for other reasons—they're lonely, they're having trouble establishing a relationship with a partner, or they're having self-realization problems which are no different from those of heterosexuals.

Question: That seems like a significant shift from the patient's viewpoint also. The gay patient comes to the therapist now with a different set of questions.

Marmor: Except that I'm not sure whether the patients who Socarides sees are the same as the patients I have been seeing. There's a certain selection that takes place between patients and their therapists. I don't doubt that there are a small minority of homosexual men who, because of their religious indoctrination or other societal attitudes, still come to psychiatrists seeking a change in their orientation.

Question: Why do you think you are different in your thinking about homosexuality from analysts like Charles Socarides, Irving Bieber, and others? Why were you able to see these things and they weren't?

Marmor: I think it came from growing up in a family with a liberal approach in general towards people who were different. I grew up with a feeling that one should be able to accept differences in people. I remember also reading Oscar Wilde's *De Profundis* and becoming interested in his life and the tragedy of a great literary talent that was destroyed by the prejudice and homophobia of that time. I remember being very moved by his "Ballad of Reading Gaol." One of its stanzas still is vivid in my memory:

> I never saw sad men who looked
> with such a wistful eye
> upon that little tent of blue
> we prisoners call the sky.
> And at every careless cloud that passed
> In happy freedom by ...

That was long before I went into psychoanalytic training. I just never believed that homosexuals were monsters or terrible people. I felt as Freud did that some of the greatest geniuses of all time have been homosexuals and contributed importantly to our society. Nevertheless, when I had my analytic training, I was led to believe that their homosexuality had been created solely by a pathogenic family background and, therefore, presumably was reversible by psychoanalytic treatment.

Question: Do you think a lot of the current shift towards a more positive attitude to gays and lesbians may be partly related to the shift in meanings about masculinity and femininity over the years? Many people often get gender and sexual orientation confused.

Marmor: There is much confusion about homosexuality and gender role behavior. The assumption that all male homosexuals are effeminate is one common misconception, and that all lesbians are butch is another. A lot of these notions are being clarified, such as the acceptance of artistic and aesthetic qualities as not being an indication of effeminacy or weakness; or the acceptance of men hugging and kissing one another. Europeans have felt freer about that much earlier than we have. I know American fathers who never kiss their sons, just shake hands. They can't show the affection that they really feel. Now, however, we are beginning to see men who are able to kiss their sons on the lips without embarrassment.

Question: Could you talk some about the process of getting the American Psychiatric Association to take homosexuality out of their diagnostic and statistical manual (the DSM-II). Weren't you President of APA at that time?

Marmor: No, I was still Vice-President. But I participated in some historical meetings with Frank Kameny and Barbara Giddings during that period. I was on one program with them at which a gay psychiatrist "came out" publicly for the first time, but only with a mask over his face and with a microphone to alter his voice. I have a photograph of that event. This was around 1971 or 1972.

This psychiatrist agreed to come on and say that he was gay but only if he were masked and if his voice was altered, because he was sure he would be fired from his position if he were recognized. He had a full-time position in a psychiatric institution. It was at that meeting that I stated I had changed my mind about things I had written in my earlier book and that I felt the psychiatric profession as a whole had to recognize the error of its ways. I pointed out how much prejudice still existed in psychiatry itself toward gays with regard to hiring them or taking them on for psychoanalytic training. I bashed my psychoanalytic colleagues for that. That was an important meeting historically.

Shortly after that a major meeting at the APA was organized where we had several thousand people in the audience. This was the first public debate about the issue of taking homosexuality out of the DSM-II as an illness. Charles Socarides, Richard Green, Bob Stoller, and I were members of the panel and it was chaired by Robert Spitzer who was chairman of the APA committee working on the new DSM-III. We debated the issue very vigorously. After that I wrote a number of papers in quick succession criticizing and attacking the mental illness theory of homosexuality.

In May of 1973, the APA Board of Trustees, after a positive recommendation from a committee that had studied the issue for a full year, passed a resolution taking homosexuality out of the DSM-III. Socarides and Bieber were furious at this decision and initiated a referendum of the entire APA membership, feeling that the membership would reject the Board's decision. I and other members of the Board did not feel that a referendum was the way to make a scientific decision. We had no choice but to go forward with the referendum. As you know, the membership supported the Board's decision and the opponents then tried to minimize the scientific decision by saying that it had been decided by a referendum. Of course, it wasn't; it was decided only after a year of careful study of the issues involved.

A subcommittee of the Research Council of the Board had studied this and then the evidence was presented to the Board. That's all been written up in Ronald Bayer's (1981) *Homosexuality and American Psychiatry*, a reasonably accurate account.

There was still another struggle afterwards because Bob Spitzer, who was chairman of the DSM-III committee, insisted on inserting a category for homosexuals who wanted to change their homosexuality, calling it "dyshomophilia." He and I had a vigorous debate about that in correspondence because I wasn't an actual member of the committee. I argued that it would result in all homosexual patients being thrown into that category and it would simply become another way of keeping homosexuality in the DSM-III.

However, it finally became "egodystonic homosexuality" with a strong disclaimer—that we insisted on—which stated that homosexuality in and of itself was not an illness. We simply couldn't get it out entirely. I was not on the DSM committee and was writing as a volunteer, so to speak. Bob Stoller felt that there ought to be such a category and he was very influential on the committee. Both Richard Green and I fought very hard against that listing. I don't think there'll be one in DSM-IV. In spite of all that, I still was elected President of APA the following year.

My argument was that if a homosexual is unhappy, if he's depressed or if he has a neurotic conflict, the diagnosis—as with heterosexual patients—should be of the underlying condition and the issue of homosexuality should not be made central to the problem. Several years later, I wrote:

> Only when we totally free ourselves from the tendency to put psychiatric labels on homosexuals that singularly differentiate them from heterosexuals with analogous problems will psychiatrists finally become free from the age-old prejudice in this area.
>
> (Marmor, 1980: 401)

We have to stop using the concept of gayness to *identify* a person. Gay people are human beings who just happen to be gay. When we treat a patient, the fact that he is gay should not become a central issue any more than the fact that he might be heterosexual. Sexuality is important but it shouldn't become the way of *defining* a person.

Question: And not all thoughts or actions, for that matter, are what you would consider a homosexual identity. The paranoid schizophrenic who has homosexual delusions isn't necessarily homosexual.

Marmor: Absolutely. Freud, with all of his good intentions, did the homosexual movement a great harm with the Schreber book, because on the basis of the Schreber case, he concluded that all paranoia was based on repressed homosexuality. It has been demonstrated over and over again that that simply is not so. Homosexual fears can be part of a paranoid delusion, but to assume that all paranoia stems from a repressed fear of homosexuality is not correct. Any sense of extreme vulnerability, whether on a sexual basis or any other basis, can lead to paranoid reactions.

For example, I just received a telephone call from a woman whose mother has become very paranoid. The elderly mother feels very vulnerable, can't remember where she places things, and has become convinced that people are stealing from her, and has begun to blame even loving relatives who are very close to her. The issue of homosexuality doesn't enter into that at all.

Question: What are your opinions then of so-called "reparative therapy?" Does it work?

Marmor: No. One of the major errors involved in so-called "cures" of homosexuality is that all that happens is that the overt *behavior* of the homosexual becomes suppressed, but the hidden homosexual *desires* and *fantasies* continue. Masters and Johnson became upset with me because I criticized their treatment of homosexuality on precisely that issue. They treated homosexuality as though it is simply a heterosexual inhibition and thought they were "curing" the condition if they enabled their patients to have heterosexual intercourse.

That's the flaw in all of these "reparative" therapies. All they succeed in doing, if they succeed, is to make possible for a man to have heterosexual intercourse if he wants to. If he's sufficiently motivated, e.g., if he wants to have children and a family, and so on, he may stick to it, but his homosexual fantasies continue. Somewhere down the line many of these men eventually leave their wives and come out as gay. And these wives have had very bad experiences.

However, we mustn't assume also that all bisexual men who get married necessarily have miserable lives. One of my bisexual friends is such a person. During his early years he was driven to seek out male companions and he would go to the parks and the "tea rooms" and would have an "experience." He was finally arrested on one occasion and very humiliated because he was a man of some status. At the same time, he had a wife he dearly loved and with whom he had several children.

However, his homosexual fantasies continued throughout his life, as did the attraction to men. To this day, even in his older years, he still has an eye for an attractive man in a way that a heterosexual man does not have. A heterosexual can admire a handsome man, but he does not feel a stirring in his loins. A homosexual man feels that stirring and it never totally disappears even though it may be suppressed.

My friend remained married and apparently still has a happy family life. Whether he would have been better off or worse off if he had become exclusively homosexual is a moot question and in any event cannot be generalized for all people one way or the other.

Question: Another issue has to do with the fact that in 1974 38 percent of the American Psychiatric Association voted against the Board's decision to remove homosexuality from the DSM-III. Since there were about 20,000 members at that time, that would leave close to 8,000 people who were really a menace to homosexuals.

Marmor: True. But I think this attitude has been gradually changing, particularly among the younger psychiatrists. Socarides is still teaching about homosexuality at Columbia and continues to be chosen to give lectures on homosexuality at the American Psychoanalytic Association meetings. It is significant that the American Psychoanalytic Association never invited me to participate in any of their panels on homosexuality. They did not want to hear any dissenting views. I think that is shocking. It's still a fairly rigid group, although they seem to be changing at long last. Even my own psychoanalytic institute in southern California turned down a man about ten years ago who was eminently qualified to be a training analyst only because he was gay. I cast a vigorous dissenting vote to the committee's decision and resigned from it after that.

Question: Could an openly gay psychiatric resident who was reasonably non-neurotic be accepted for psychoanalytic training today?

Marmor: That's a good question and I don't know the answer to it. I think there are some institutes in which he would be accepted. I think it depends upon the people in charge of the selection process. The American Academy of Psychoanalysis and now even the American Psychoanalytic have both made clear-cut statements that the existence of homosexuality in an applicant should not influence his being chosen as a candidate or a training analyst. They have a nondiscrimination clause. But since the whole selection process is so secretive, you really still can't always know what actually transpires.

There's a little bit of history that you may be interested in with regard to this issue. When I broke with the American Psychoanalytic Association originally over the issue of academic freedom and Karen Horney, I joined her group. Then, she refused to give Erich Fromm training analyst status on the ground that he was not an M.D., although he had already been a well-established psychoanalyst and member of the International Psychoanalytic Association. I and others felt she was trying to form a "Horney group" which was against the very principle of academic freedom on which we had broken away. So, several of us split off from the Horney group and formed the first psychoanalytic institute in the United States under the aegis of a medical school at New York Medical College. This was 1942.

The man we picked as the president of the new psychoanalytic society was Dr. William Silverberg, who we all knew was gay. He had been married and had left his wife some years previously. He was living openly with a young man who was his lover, and we all respected him as a wonderful human being and an outstanding psychoanalyst.

We didn't look at him negatively in the New York Medical College group. We knew him personally, recognized him as a solid individual and good psychoanalyst. We just ignored it. We made no issue of it. We knew he was an able and honorable man, and we respected him enough to make him the first president of the New York Society of Medical Psycho-analysts.

Question: Right now, we are hearing a debate about gays in the military. What do you think is going to happen with this issue?

Marmor: Clinton has got to do something about it. First of all he has a genuine obligation to the gay community, who played a big part in his election. You know, the same arguments, the identical arguments, almost word for word, were made at the time President Truman said the military would have to accept blacks: "you've got to be able to trust the man in a foxhole next to you," "you've got to be able to sleep in the same bunkhouse, shower together, etc." When Truman finally made it a mandate, within months blacks and whites were buddies, fighting side by side. The same thing will happen when gays are admitted to the military without prejudice.

Prejudice is prejudice. People who hated blacks didn't want to use the same toilet with a black man. Once you start living with people as people, however, these distorted feelings begin to disappear. Gays are an integrated part of the military in half a dozen European countries already.

Question: In many ways you're a hero to many gay and lesbian people. When you look back at your career, what things jump out to you? Are you proud to have been so associated with these issues and changes?

Marmor: Oh, absolutely. I wouldn't have done it otherwise. I did it because I thought it was right, not because I thought I'd be honored by the gay community. It is one of the things in which I definitely do take some great satisfaction.

Also, you know, I've been a rebel about psychoanalytic theory, in general. I was one of the early people to question the libido theory and to recognize the importance of a bio-psycho-social approach and a systems theory approach to psychoanalysis as well as other forms of psychiatry. I was "boycotted" by the American Psychoanalytic Association, not primarily for my views on homosexuality, but for my views on psychoanalytic theory.

However, I still became a member of the Association because I decided I could fight for the things I believed in more effectively from within the organization than outside of it. When I came to California in 1947, I joined the regular psychoanalytic society and was readmitted to the American Psychoanalytic after a period of "penance" that involved undergoing additional supervision with Drs. Martin Grotjahn and May Romm.

I wrote my "graduation thesis" in 1948. Come to think of it, that paper was interesting because it ties in with some of the things we have been talking about. It was about a Jew who disowned his Jewishness and went around beating up other Jews and why he disowned his own minority status. That was the "thesis" that I presented for "graduation" and acceptance into membership in the local society and subsequently into the American Psychoanalytic.

I worked with that patient in New York City. He used to go to Brooklyn and beat up elderly Jews on the streets. Although he didn't call himself a Nazi, he admired Hitler. He was not a homosexual. He hated his father. He had a brutal father over whom he triumphed by identifying with Hitler, the "aggressor," and then beating up the elderly Jews who symbolized his father.

Several years later, I became one of the founders of the American Academy of Psychoanalysis and that became my analytic home. There we have tolerance for all points of view, and everybody is free to speak his mind. That is what a scientific group should be like. That's something to which I'm dedicated. I take pride in that. It has always been one of the credos that have guided me.

Part II

Life stories of some gay men

Chapter 5

An introduction to the interviews

> The life history is experienced as a journey to one's current place.
>
> (Connell, 1992: 746)

A study of life stories or biographies is often a study of how people construct and reconstruct the meaning of their past experiences in light of their present situations and identities. All human beings attempt to make sense of their world. By delving into the past, we find themes and events that give meaning to present lives. In other words, we create our own past; we construct our own biographies; we make our own meanings. As Berger (1963:56) phrases it, "we ourselves go on interpreting and reinterpreting our own life. ... As we remember the past, we reconstruct it in accordance with our present ideas of what is important and what is not."

However, the memories we conjure up and the specific events we recollect are heavily influenced by cultural and social contexts. Memories of early family life, for example, can evoke very different images at the ages of 15, 30, or 60. At each point in life, we make interpretations and we develop themes which help make sense out of past experiences and create new meanings for the present ones. Stories are often reconstructed and reinterpreted as people change from one world view to another, that is, as they enter careers, leave home, retire, begin or end relationships, or "come out." In short, people retell their stories and "the discrepant fragments of their biography [are ordered] in a meaningful theme" (Berger, 1963: 62).

The use of biography as a source for understanding people is a research methodology that has often been ignored or maligned as not scientific enough. Yet, autobiographical "life documents are an immensely valuable and vastly under-rated source" (Plummer, 1983: 11) because they provide data typically not generated by other more traditional scientific means. As Plummer (1983: 14) forcefully argues about life histories:

It does not matter if the account can later be shown to be false in particulars—most accounts, even so-called "scientific" ones, are context-bound and speak to certain people, times and circumstances. What matters, therefore, in life history research is the facilitation of as full a subjective view as possible, not the naive delusion that one has trapped the bedrock of truth. Given that most social science seeks to tap the "objective," the life history reveals, like nothing else can, the subjective realm.

Life stories are also heavily influenced by those asking questions with particular assumptions, knowledge, and cultural information. Which story we tell depends on who poses the query and how it is asked. This is especially the case for gay people, like the men interviewed in this project. Their life stories are their versions of the past as recollected from a perspective of a gay identity in the years 1978 and 1979, as framed by the interviewer's questions and assumptions. How gay men and lesbians recall their past typically depends on what the gender and sexual orientation roles of the present are and what the current "knowledge about the antecedents (or commonly anticipated antecedents) of a homosexual orientation" is (Ross, 1980: 524). Perhaps other stories would have been told and other questions asked if they were interviewed in 1984, for example, after AIDS became an important concern; or in 1964, years before the modern gay and women's liberation movements introduced different political, social, and psychological meanings to the concepts of "homosexual," "femininity," and "masculinity."

Biography is not simply a fixed list of facts, dates, and events. It is a story developed at a particular time and place, selectively chosen from all possible past experiences. Certain events are highlighted, specific stories are remembered, just as others are passed over, selectively reworked, or forgotten. In another place, at another time, other details might be told and recalled. As Blum (1981: 294) phrased it: "there is, in this process, no 'truth'; at best, even using conventional empirical methods, one achieves approximations of what a person is or was 'really like'."

We often seek continuities even when they may not be there. We strive to make sense of the present and we do—by finding the past events which give meaning to and shape the present identity. The past is the use of "facts [to] argue the developmental meaning of the present" (Gubrium and Buckholdt, 1977: 164). As the present changes—both personally and socio-politically—so does the past.

Much of what is communicated in a life story depends on the inter-action with the person recording the story. What people tell a lover, a parent, a therapist, or a friend about their past may vary depending on the person listening. How the question is posed, which questions are asked, and the reactions of the interviewer all contribute to the answers given.

In the process of disclosing the past to another, people reconstruct experiences differently depending on their own current sense of self, the interviewer, and the setting. Freeman and Krantz (1980: 6) believe that "a narrator's life history might well become recognizably different if it were collected by a different person with a different personal background and different categories of reference to guide his directing and editing the narrator's account." It is not only the "objective facts" of life that are recorded but also the meanings and interpretations of those facts by both the interviewer and the interviewed.

Life stories, or biographies, are an inquiry into identity. McAdam (1985: 25, 57) argues that during adolescence, people become biographers of self: "identity is conceived as a life story which provides unity and purpose in human lives. ... Identity is a life story which individuals begin constructing, consciously and unconsciously, in late adolescence." And when that identity goes through significant changes, as when gay men and lesbians "come out," the power of telling stories about one's life, in the present and in the past, becomes evident (see Hall Carpenter Archives, 1989a and 1989b).

What follows, then, is an interpretation and organization of eleven gay men's life stories. Their biographies reflect a collaboration of several different people at different times and places. These men have given meanings to events in their past filtered through their gay identity and American gay subculture in 1979. They reflect the kinds of questions asked by David Sanders, a psychiatrist, and developed with psychiatrist Judd Marmor, working under a prevalent model of that decade that sought to understand homosexuality by probing into parental–child relations, gender-nonconforming childhood activities, and sexual activities in an age before AIDS. The stories reflect the editing of Peter Nardi, a sociologist, organizing the material in 1983 by making decisions about what to include or exclude, in part based on what issues were being discussed at that period in history.

These life stories, therefore, are not meant to be representative of all gay people and certainly not representative of lesbians' stories. They are of a particular set of white, middle- to upper-middle-class American males, who lived and worked in large urban coastal cities in the late 1970s, and who grew up and "came out" in the decades before the 1969 Stonewall rebellion—the impetus to and the symbol of the modern gay liberation movements.

Although they come from a variety of American rural and urban locations, grew up in different social classes and in different white ethnic and religious backgrounds, these men in no way illustrate the diversity of experiences that gay men and lesbians live. They were purposely selected to demonstrate how psychologically healthy, middle-age white gay men negotiated their personal, professional, and sexual lives in their past and in the present.

What we offer, then, are their life stories as told in a particular historical time and place, in response to a specific set of social and psychological questions, for the purpose of illuminating how some people were able to deal successfully with life and its many complexities, while growing up in an age before gay liberation and coming out in an era before AIDS.

Chapter 6

Andrew
Sexual childhood and separate bedrooms

Andrew is a 50 year old Texan who has been teaching at a small college for many years after having been fired from an earlier teaching job in 1953 for being gay. He was born in 1927 and his early childhood memories primarily revolve around his grandparents and their strong influence on his life. Andrew's childhood was, also, highly sexual and he recounts many stories about those experiences with adult men and his male and female cousins, his infatuation with World War II soldiers, and his "coming out" in the 1950s. He and his lover have been together twenty years. Although they maintain separate bedrooms now and separate sexual lives, Andrew believes they are mated for life.

FAMILY MEMORIES

My father died in 1948. However, there was a divorce in my family when I was six years of age and I was not reared in any way around my father. The father figure in my childhood was my grandfather, my mother's father. My mother is still alive—a very old, senile woman. I knew my father until I was 6 and I saw him again for maybe thirty minutes fourteen or fifteen years later when I was in college.

My real father was a complete womanizer. He was married six times in his lifetime. He married my mother when she was 35 and he had a family of eight children, for which my mother served as mother for the six years that they were married. These children, during the first six years of my life, had a very strong influence on me. They were from age 10 through 20 to 25—they were grown. I can remember particularly the oldest of the boys, who turned out to be gay, used to take me riding on his motorcycle and I can remember that experience—that's before I was 6.

After my father left my mother he had invented a type of engine for which he was paid some extraordinary amount of money. He ran off with a woman who was a Northern woman. This was during Prohibition and my father left her and married two or three times, until every bit of the money that he had was just totally dissipated, and he died in a mental institution. The man totally dissipated himself according to what I can gather, but you have to remember that my father essentially deserted his children and my mother never allowed me to forget that. One season she would speak out in fondness and then the next season she was denouncing him for having deserted us, and I think he was always more a legend in my mind. For many, many years when I was a child, from the age of 8 until I was 15, I always had fantasies of my father sending me a Lionel electric train for Christmas. We had no electricity, we had kerosene lamps. I'd ordered the Lionel catalogues every year and went through great fantasies on this Lionel train, and this great mythical figure who had money, who I would write letters to every Christmas. I can't remember if any of those letters were every mailed. I can't remember that I ever mailed them. First of all, we didn't have money for postage stamps.

When I finally met him again, it was under very adverse conditions. The oldest son, who was gay, had been killed in World War II and we were all gathered as a family on the night before the funeral, and he was such a broken, debilitated man—he was an alcoholic. He'd already had one of his strokes. And he was there with his last wife. I think I looked on him as just a totally broken, defeated man.

My grandfather was a grand benevolent man—accepting of everything and everyone. He had been a cowboy in Texas and he had seen and experienced everything. He was a very powerful, generous man. Many people in the community thought he was gullible because he never turned anybody down for an appeal for help. He loved people and he loved a wide variety of people. He was a very important influence in my religious training—very stern Protestant sect—peculiar to the Texas environment. He never really paid much attention to it, although ostensibly he was a member of this same group. It was a group called the Church of Christ—they make Baptists look very liberal. But anyway, he never took it very seriously, and I think that was a fundamental part of my childhood outlook of what was around me.

He had been a cowboy until he settled down. He homesteaded there in Texas and after that he was a rancher and farmer—raised a large family in the old homeplace and that was where I grew up. He had been a relatively wealthy man until the depression in 1929 and he had been a director of a bank that went under. My grandfather voluntarily paid off every person who lost anything in the bank. The end result was that in the Depression years of the '30s he was land poor. He hadn't a penny and we lived under conditions that would be far more poverty level than almost anything you can conceive, and when he died in 1941 he left the land—divided it up between his ten children and my mother got her one-tenth, which she eventually sold in order to keep us alive. We had to have food.

I was extraordinarily close to him. You see, I'm so keenly interested in Greek, both ancient and modern, and this stems directly from his influence. He had gone to a seminary prior to the Civil War in which he had learned vast sections of the *Iliad* in ancient Greek, and we'd be riding along on a horse—I'd be behind him—he'd start quoting passages from the *Iliad* in Greek, and I heard it as a child and grew to love it. But I didn't develop this until the last fifteen or twenty years. It's a relatively late development.

If I could say what his attitude toward sex was I'd have to project a great deal because I don't think my grandfather ever discussed sex in any way with me. We were on the ranch with endless sexual situations with the cattle and with the horses, and it was just a part of everyday life, and there were a few years when I had to participate in taking care of the breeding among the stock. My grandfather never said a word to me. But it was just a participatory learning. And I believe that my grandfather had probably had many same-sex experiences when he had been a cowboy, because I know that he was extraordinarily fond of two of the men with whom he had rode herd in the ten or twelve years when he was riding from South Texas to Kansas. I believe that my grandfather may never have had a word for what his relationship was with those men, but if he had known or he were to know today that I'm gay, I think he would have accepted it, without any question.

My mother is still in Texas, but she left the old homeplace. The old house burned in 1946—a very important fact in my life. I had already left home to go away to college and I knew that I was leaving it forever, but the burning of the house effectively made it impossible for me to return—it was a very good thing. It uprooted my mother, a lost woman. She likewise has married repeatedly. She was born in 1892, she married again in 1941—so that would make her—yes, about 50 when she married again, and then after she lived a life of misery with that second husband, with whom she shared nothing except hostility. Oh, she was miserable. Then after he died she married again—one of her old childhood sweethearts someone she had known when she was a teenager. Then he died after a year or so, and then she married again to a man who lived six months—she's always believed that she needed a man as a breadwinner.

She was a very fond and loving person, who would have sacrificed anything for her two children, my sister and me, and she did sacrifice a great deal. She always gave us preferential treatment from childhood on up, and I know that she gave me preferential treatment over my sister, but she was an uneducated woman. She had no conception of what was occurring in my sister and me because we were already beginning to separate ourselves from that rural Texas background, and she supported me in all of this separation—she supported my interests and encouraged them, but she knew nothing of what she was encouraging. She knew that I was fantasizing of going to college; she knew I was writing for catalogues, but she had no conception of what this meant. She encouraged it.

I used mother in my childhood as my defender. I allowed her to be the shield in all relationships and I learned that using her as a shield only discredited me in my conflicts, and I began to lose respect for her. For all intents and purposes, my mother died for me in the 1950s—she's lived twenty more years, and I'm actually indifferent to her. She refuses at the age of 86 to go into a nursing home. She's hardly able to walk, and if that's her decision, I say OK—if she falls and breaks her hip and dies after no one seeing her for three or four days, she had made the choice—that's the way I approach that. My sister feels much more guilty about it than I do. I don't feel any guilt. I send her money regularly, but she loses the money.

Some of the people at their church drop by to see her occasionally—I really don't know how she's surviving. I've gone back there every two, three or four years and done everything I can to persuade her to go into a nursing home where someone can take care of her, but she refuses, and as a consequence I've said, "I'm not going to force you."

I have a sister who's four years younger. She and I were together throughout our childhood. There was a cousin, a female cousin who was approximately the same age I was. She had a very strong influence on me in adolescence. You have no idea of the isolation of which I'm speaking. We were 15 miles from anyone, and so I had to learn to entertain myself. School was small. We had a one-room school with all eleven grades and it was on my grandfather's land, but it was 11 miles away, and there were few, if any, cars. There were maybe ten or twelve students in the school for all the grades, so there were no real peers at the school. We never had enough for a basketball team.

My sister is a lesbian. I found out that she was gay when we were in Paris together. She was in the WACS and I was in school. This was in 1953. I had known from college years that my sister showed all the earmarks of being a lesbian. However, I didn't approach her on it. I knew she was having deeply passionate relationships with some of her female friends. We were just living off of one another on a shoestring. I can remember outside Paris I confronted her with it. And she acknowledged that she had known that I was gay—of course, she had to know because she knew that I had been fired from a teaching job because I was gay. She acknowledged that she had known about herself and acknowledged that she had known about me and we went through about ten years of being very, very close, and we're still close but we never get in touch with each other but about once every two or three months, because she's living her full and complete life in Texas and I'm living mine here.

My grandmother also was on the ranch. She died in 1938 and she was a very, very, stern, cold, unloving person. During the years that she was alive she was the person we had to avoid. My mother had never gotten along with her own mother, and so we just evaded her as much as possible. I don't think I've ever known anyone to play favorites as much as she did. She began collecting candy in her last years—she got very senile in her 80s—and I can remember sitting in front of the fireplace late in the evening. She would go in and get some of the candy out of this huge big chest and she would sit there in front of me, and she would offer some to my grandfather, who usually turned it down. She would never offer any to my mother. Then she would ask my sister and me, if we wanted any of the candy, and of course we always said yes, and then she would say "but you're not gonna get it." She was a fantastic woman. We just stayed out of her way. There was plenty of room. The house was a huge thing with about twenty-five rooms and we would stay upstairs if she was down in the main part of the house, or we'd be out, miles away.

EARLY SOCIAL EXPERIENCES

I have very weak eyes, so weak that all my life, I've never been able to drive. I don't think I was ever told the truth by my mother about my weak eyes, but she was always telling me stories about experiences when I was very young. Frequently, she tried to ascribe my weak eyes to this or my weak eyes to that, and the most frequently repeated story was a story that I crawled into a bedroom of one of my aunts and ate some bichloride of mercury which this woman had in her suitcase. The thing that saved me from having died was that we lived just a few blocks from the hospital and I'd eaten some heavy greased gravy for breakfast and I vomited all this up, but they felt that I was dead. Now my mother told me from the time I first recall, that I had weak eyes because of the bichloride of mercury poison. I never questioned that. Frankly, I don't know whether it can be true or not.

My eyes are so weak that the first diagnosis which I had of them was when I was what would have been called the fifth grade. They were about

20–600 in the left eye and about 20–400 or 20–500 in the right eye. My teachers in that little school had known that my eyes were weak, but I never really knew it. I never had glasses until I was 12 years of age. I just knew that I couldn't see if we ever played games with a ball. I couldn't play in the games because I couldn't see unless it was such a game as jumping rope or something like that sort of thing I could do. It never really dawned on me until one of the teachers in the school, when I was 12, paid out of her own pocket to get me some glasses and the world was transformed for me. The best they could get was a correction of about 20–200—I can get a correction today of about 20–60—but that transformed my life. I had read and read and read with a book right in front of my face all those years and I learned that I could read holding the book at pretty much of a normal distance. But I was never able to participate in anything that involved quick-sightedness.

My mother always blamed my father for my weak eyes—gave me endless stories about how my great-uncles had never been able to serve in the Civil War because they had weak eyes. So she attributed it either to the bichloride of mercury poisoning or to a genetic defect on the side of my father's family. She never in her entire training of me ever acknowledged such things as it could have been a dietary deficiency on her part during the pregnancy period—I do not know. I've never been able to get an answer why my eyes have been so weak.

But it's turned out one of the most important factors in my life. It was a crucial factor in my coming to San Francisco. I had to choose a city that had a good public transportation system. I couldn't have gone to a city such as Houston or Los Angeles, where if you don't drive you're lost. Throughout my life I have known indirectly that my weak eyes have been a very important factor in decisions I've had to make.

The most important thing in my adolescence was when I began writing a novel at 14 years of age. I was just absolutely sure that this novel was going to transform the world. I had no concept of what the world was like, I just knew that it was going to transform the world. You have no idea how preposterous it was. But the point that I'm trying to make, is that the novel was rejected by Macmillan Company Publishers, with sound, sound reasoning. It nearly destroyed me. It was the biggest crisis of my life. I would have been 16 or 17. And that I survived that is something I do not fully understand. It was the greatest period of depression of my life, and if I hadn't had the experience and the knowledge that I had survived that, I don't think I could have survived what occurred in 1953 when I was fired from a teaching job.

EARLY SEXUAL MEMORIES

I was very active sexually as a boy. I remember being involved with some boys who I was playing with who were the same age as I was, about 5, prior to my being uprooted from one part of Texas to go to another part. One of my earliest sexual experiences was with this boy. He and I began playing together and we constructed sand mounds in which we constructed penises. We played with these; we enjoyed this very much and we played with one another.

Now after my parents' divorce in 1934, we were uprooted and moved out to the ranch, then my sexual experiences were entirely different. I began getting very involved sexually with a lot of the animals on the ranch. I remember particularly being endlessly fascinated with one of the stallions that we had. I was just enamored of that stallion. Every time the stallion would piss I would just stand transfixed, and when the stallion would encounter one of the mares in heat, one of the things that my grandfather and I always had to do was to help the stallion get his cock into the mare. Very seldom can they do it. I would get so excited I could just hardly contain myself. And then later on we had no bulls—after we got so poor we had only milk cows—we had no bull and we had to "take the cow off", and what this meant was when the cow was in heat we had to take the cow to one of the neighbors who had a bull and we had to go through the whole process. I remember one time my grandfather and I took one of our guernsey cows to one of the neighbors who had a very young bull and the bull was so young that it was very small in relation to the cow. We had to put the cow with her front feet in the trailer—sloping—and had to dig a trench so that the bull could actually copulate with the cow. I was fascinated with all of this.

There was a great deal of sexuality all around me and I was very, very sexual in my interests. I was already masturbating at this time, although of course there was no ejaculation—I was already having orgasms. I can remember we had a man who came through and worked for a period of about six weeks or longer. He and I became very sexually involved with a great deal of same-sex activity. I was probably 8—making a guess—and frankly I loved that man, and when he left it just broke me up.

He would play with me, I would play with him. That was my first time to see an adult male cock, and that's when I first sucked anyone off. We never got into any anal intercourse, but it was an entirely positive experience, and he was such a loving, and nurturing person. I grew so fond of him that I waited for him to return for two or three years. What he was was a hobo passing through, a Depression hobo, who worked on the farm.

Oh, I learned a lot of things from him. I learned how to plow in a straight line. He helped—we gave him food, you see—and he slept in the barn and that's when I began going up to the barn—began to identify the barn with sexual experiences.

Now this is where my cousin Lydia begins to enter. She was about a year older than I was. And she and my sister and I would go on fishing trips. She lived about a mile from us. Lydia was very involved sexually. She had access to the family car. She was seeing many of the boys who lived within 5 to 10 miles. My sister, Lydia, and I would go on fishing trips together. We'd usually spend the night. We'd go to a place where we could get catfish. It was Lydia who first began to initiate me into fucking women. She and I fucked regularly, from the time I was about 9 until I was 16. This was frequent, two or three times a week, and it was Lydia who was always the aggressor in this. I don't think I ever voluntarily started it. She always started it; I always participated.

Then, when the war years came along, there was an army plant about 20 miles away. Her father and mother, my aunt and uncle, were raising trucking produce on their farmland and two or three times a week they would take this trucking produce into town and sell it. They would take Lydia and me and she would walk the streets and pick up oh, four or five soldiers and they would carry them back out in the truck to the ranch and these four or five soldiers would spend the weekend out there at the ranch. Lydia would fuck every one of them. By that time, I was stopping the sexual activity with her, but instead, I was in love with every one of the soldiers that she was bringing out there.

I had the biggest crushes on them you ever saw. I can remember Christmastime one year, this must have been 1944, the year I graduated from school. Lydia was getting Christmas presents for all of her soldier boyfriends and I was so enamored of them all. I was likewise stealing eggs and selling eggs in order to get money to give Christmas presents to all these soldiers who I had just met and ridden with in the back of the truck.

Sex was pleasurable, but it was never the sort of sex that involved anything more than what I can call "gonadal release." There was no emotional involvement in it. A lot of my male cousins who were my age or older would occasionally come to the homeplace and spend two or three days, or sometimes even longer than that. Sometimes I would sleep with them in one of the bedrooms upstairs, and sometimes I was in another bedroom, depending on how many people we would have there. I would always enjoy when they'd get so many that I would have to end up sleeping with someone, because in every one of those cases I ended up seducing the older cousins in bed. It usually amounted to nothing more than masturbation—mutual masturbation, but I was the aggressor in every one of these cases. I must tell you that I tried everything sexually as a child—with the cattle, with the calves, with the pigs, with the passing hobos, with all of my cousins, male and female—and I never felt guilty about it—I only felt that it was something that I shouldn't talk about. Somehow I knew that it was not to be talked about.

I can remember when I was baptized in this Church of Christ, there was a boy I had a crush on who was to be baptized along with me, and while we were waiting to be baptized—you know, the real dunking kind of baptism—we were waiting in one of the little back rooms of the church. I started playing with him and sucked his cock. I can remember that just as clear—I approached everyone sexually.

I didn't put a name to my homosexuality until I was about 20 years of age. I was well along in college before I had any name. The name I got was homosexuality, and I got that from the library at the college where I was going. It produced a measure of anxiety. I went through a great period of anxiety from about the age of 18 until about the age of 25, because I was having to apply what I found the social matrix wanted me to think concerning all of my sexual activities, and you see, I had been pretty much exempted from that. It wasn't until I really got into, I can call it the outside world—that's literally what it was—that I found out that you couldn't just be that open in your sexual approaches.

It was a sternly religious college and one of the first things I began to learn was that all aspects of sex were regarded as either unmentionable or at best to be lauded to the skies in matrimonial bliss, and so all aspects of sex became dangerous and nasty. I never thought that, never really felt that. I'd always known a kind of furtive quality about sex because I'd always had to be very active and aggressive in seduction. Wordless, because I had no words for what I was doing, but when I began to get external attitudes imposed upon me I felt very, very troubled by it for the period of time. Once I pretty much picked the dust of the Church of Christ off my heels. I never really was troubled by guilt from that time on, which was about the age of 25 around 1952.

The first time I really encountered a sexual experience in which I was put in a very embarrassing situation was I guess about 1944, when I was about 16 or 17. I'd gone to a movie. The cinema was packed, with soldiers. It was a small movie theater but there must have been ten people in the theater who were not soldiers. They had what were called love seats in those days, in which two people had to sit together without an arm in between them, and I ended up being put into one of the love seats and a soldier sat in the love seat with me. He began to play kneesies with me and I'd never encountered this before. He invited me to go back to the men's room and in the men's room he was jacking me off and I was jacking him off. One of the ushers in the theater came in and I can remember that we were ordered out of the theater, or out onto the street, and it really upset me, because something had happened there that had never happened to me before. There had never been a word exchanged between me and this soldier, but I couldn't believe that any person could have felt as furtive about it as he seemed to be feeling. He was just totally demoralized by what occurred to him and that impressed me.

I began in college assuming that I could continue all of the sexual activity that I had had earlier, but I found out in that stern religious environment that sex was just not to be a part of my life. So during my college years I had virtually no sexual experience whatsoever. I did have a lot of crushes—never any overt sexual activity, and by the time I had graduated from college I can say I was living as a hermit sexually speaking, although I was still having strong crushes.

When I went away to college, one of the first encounters I had was with a junior or senior and he seemed such a suave, sophisticated person coming from the outside world. He latched on to me and became very, very close to me and within a week's time I was clearly convinced that we were going to end up in bed together. He invited me to go to dinner with him. He seemed to have a lot of money, I had no money, and I remember he took me to a hotel and I had shrimp. I'd never heard of shrimp in my life. We had shrimp and he wanted me to spend the night with him, and he had a tiny, little narrow bed and I just assumed that this would mean sexual activity. He decided he would sleep on the floor and I would sleep on the bed. I was just brokenhearted, and when I tried to approach him sexually, he was horrified and asked that we pray together. That established a pattern. I had never seen anything that was to me explicit as a sexual come-on in which he wanted us to do everything together—but the moment that anything sexual became involved in it ... I was frustrated you see—and so all of what I will call my aggressive tendencies that had existed in earlier years diminished to such a point that I stopped becoming an aggressor at any time, and that was to remain my pattern until pretty close to the age of 30 in the late 1950s.

CURRENT SITUATION AND EXPERIENCES

My lover and I met one another just about that time. We've been together twenty years, and during the early years of our relationship it was pretty much of a monogamous relationship in which he demanded total

exclusivity. I had never been that devoted to a totally exclusive arrangement, but I went along with it. I allowed him to essentially control it
because he seemed to need that very, very much. He needed that measure
of security, and I was certainly never the aggressor during those early
years of our relationship, because he set up conditions for all of our sexual
activity. However, I began, about ten or twelve years ago, to assert myself
sexually in the relationship, demanding that the relationship go through
some mutations.

Our relationship, any relationship that has lasted as long as ours has,
has had to change. You cannot have a museum-piece relationship. It
continued to go through mutations through the years, because it's a living
thing. I began to assert myself far more and it turned out to be very good
for both of us. Our relationship now cannot be classified as anything other
than a beautiful relationship in which we go our own ways primarily for
all sexual activity, but we are, I suppose, mated for life. There will never
be any question about that, I don't believe.

We do not now have sex with each other. We have separate bedrooms,
although we frequently do sleep together. We may begin again, but he is
so busy sexually, and I have been so busy sexually, I don't know how we
could work one another in, sexually, right now.

He regularly brings his friends here, and some of them go over long
periods of time. He becomes very fond of them, but I hardly ever bring
anyone here, and almost all of my sexual activity now is in the summers
when I go to Greece. When I come here, I usually have very limited sexual
contact, except with people who are very near and dear. I hardly ever have
what I would call one-night stands anymore. But in Greece I'm totally
promiscuous. I can see that that's going through changes. I've been going
there now since the late 1960s.

Frequently we take vacations together. He was in Greece last year
along with me, and we were together while we were there. We cruised
separately, we never cruised together. It's not that it's threatening, it's just
that we don't cruise in the same places.

I really and truly enjoy sex for sex's sake today, in which everything
goes. If the relationship becomes something in which it is more than just
sex, we become close friends—that's alright. I'm never threatened by that.
But I really and truly enjoy just sex for sex's sake, without any feelings
of the tension that I knew in those somewhat furtive things when I was a
child, or the tensions that existed in the following years when everyone
was jockeying for position and looking for lovers and so forth. I've really
enjoyed sex more in the last ten years than I have any time since childhood.

Around 1972, I came out on campus. Initially at that time, many of the people who had known me over the years tended to be a little ill at ease. That didn't bother me, I just let them deal with their own discomfort. But increasingly, I found out that it's distinctly to my advantage to be out, not only as a teacher, but also in my few relationships with my colleagues. I have been supported at great length by my colleagues, both straight and gay—no, I cannot say I've been supported by my gay colleagues who are closeted. They are the ones who now tend to run from me as an openly gay person.

It's been the best thing for my teaching that ever occurred. I've always been a good teacher, and for many years I was the chair of the personnel committee, involved in hiring about sixty people on our faculty, and had been out as a gay person, even in the hiring procedures, and I've learned a lot about what closets do. I've seen in the hiring procedure that the closets wither and kill. I've had nothing but support for my own well-being in my relationships with others, and increasingly I believe I have made the right decision.

I can say I am a happy person. But there were long stretches in my life when I was not. When I was fired in 1953, I went through the most critical period of my life. This was in my mid-20s. And at that time, by the way, I would seriously have considered suicide. I'm sure I would. What I've done all my life is close doors on the past. When I leave a thing, I leave it. You know the pattern of burning of the house? When I left Texas, I left Texas. When I left school, I left school. When I left college, I left it. I've never gone back. And so therefore, I can essentially say that the pattern of the last twenty years during which my lover and I have been here together and did this house over, when I closed the door on our monogamous period—I closed that door. And I don't know what other doors I'll close in the future, but if a thing holds unpleasant aspects, I think I can deal with it.

Chapter 7

Bennett
Sissy boy, teenage crushes, and choices

Ben is a 40 year old professor of philosophy born in Colorado in 1939. He is not involved with a lover although he has just begun a new relationship. Ben is a reflective and philosophical person as can be seen in his discussions about his early life and recent relationships. His sexual confusion is evident as he fools around with other teenage boys in the late 1950s, falls in love with a straight boy, becomes engaged to women, drinks too much, and finally learns in the late 1960s to choose what he really feels. His concern focuses on his ability to form an ongoing relationship and on making the right choices in his life for the right reasons.

FAMILY MEMORIES

My father is an alcoholic. I mean in the kind of sense that every once in a while he goes on binges and drinks. He builds up every couple of months and dries out and doesn't drink for a while, but that's kind of been true for a long time now. And so he struggles with that. But for the most part he seems to have things under control. He's a lot mellower now than he was. He had about eight brothers and sisters. His mother died in the birth of the last brother. And his father as far as I can tell was really something of a religious fanatic. Both were Mormons. My father was about 16 or 17 I believe when the economic pinch came after World War I. My father's father killed himself right in the barn in front of my father and took cyanide, leaving my father, the eldest at that time. His older brother had been killed by a horse, so he was the only one left, and he lost the ranch. And the children were all farmed out to relatives and I don't know what really happened to him after that for fifteen years. By the time he met my mother and got married, he was about 30 at the time.

My mother was really quite a catch I guess for him. From then on, he was very much involved with and dedicated to creating a financially secure foundation for the family. They didn't have children for six years after they were married. I think the reasons for that, during the Depression, were probably financial. Anyway, kids finally came along, my brother was born three years before I was, then me, and then my sister.

He's quite a remarkable person in terms of just his perseverance, stubbornness in doing what he had to do. The cost, however, was really enormous. His attention really was on dealing with the cold, cruel world outside. He just didn't have much time for any of us. I can give you a measure of how distant we all were. My sister, largely because of my father's jealousy of her involvement with boys, was driven into getting married, by him. She married at the age of 16. She did that pretty clearly to get away from him.

My brother really had a lot of problems, too. I think they were largely because my father came to make judgments on my brother. My brother was lazy and incompetent and wouldn't do what he was supposed to, wouldn't get out and work, and he wouldn't do his work in school. In fact, the total effect on my brother was for him to really give up in school. In high school he flunked lots of courses. He was always stocky as a child and simply found what refuge he had in obesity. He is still now a very obese person. He managed eventually to get through college, but only after a long period of time with lots of failures and a sense of worthlessness on his part. My father managed to give him a real sense of his own incompetence.

Although he didn't attack me about school, that was the good part, it was only when I finally got my Ph.D. that my father really came around and he liked that. I mean, my gosh, you really did do something. Of course, by that time a lot of the pressure was off, too. The financial pressure was off, the kids were all away, and he'd become a much more mellow person. By that time he'd had a bad ulcer cut out. And so this recurrent pain in that regard was gone. That changed him a lot, he was a lot mellower after that.

He used to discipline us with a strap, with his belt. Sometimes I didn't expect it. One time my mother had made this great ham and she was taking a nap so we started picking at it and before we knew it we had eaten a lot of it. She was angry; she said, "Wait 'til your father gets home." For some reason when my father got home, we were all joking about it, all laughing and so forth. By God, he just sort of let off and gave us a whipping.

We both put up with one another now. The family gets together maybe once every year, year and a half; three kids and my father and his new wife. We deal with one another and I think it's uncomfortable for all of us for different reasons. But I think he's bothered about it because I think he feels like he did something wrong with all of us. And I think it's a source of guilt, or maybe just, I don't know what it is. The tendency to drink a lot usually comes in anticipation of these gatherings which he, however, insists upon. He's definitely the motivating force behind them. I could feel affectionately toward him. He's been good to me ever since we've been growing up. I mean I could do without spending time with him.

At the time it was clear that he had a really bad thing about jealousy of my sister. He would go into rages in which he would complain about her being a prostitute or going around sleeping with all the boys. I don't think my sister actually ever slept with any of them. But he read that into it. When they'd come to the door to see her or anything, he would chew them out, or tell them off.

One time my mother and my father went out to dinner some place. My sister and I were home alone. We were prepubescent. We decided to sleep together and so we were in my sister's bed, not doing much at all really, but when my father got home and found us there he was outraged. I mean he was so angry, it would seem like for no cause at all. We were just laying there, in bed together. We hadn't really gotten around to fooling around. He didn't know that; he had no ground for it.

Father was clearly the authority figure for all manifest purposes. And he was the one that made decisions and we always had to consult my father. He was the disciplined one, he was the one that made decisions about when we went on vacation and all that sort of stuff. But as a matter of fact the reality was that my mother made those decisions and in a sense was manipulating him. I have no evidence that he knew that he was being manipulated. My impression is that she married beneath herself.

They always kissed when they parted, it was a pro forma sort of thing. My mother was very affectionate. Maybe especially towards me. But my father was not inclined to express his affection bodily. I think what I get from my father is my discipline. If I have to and I decide I want to, I can force myself to do the most outrageous, painful things for as long a period as is necessary. That's what I got from my father. For example, the whole school thing was part of it. Lots of times it was simply a matter of sheer discipline. And time and time again I found myself in situations where I had to do things I didn't want to do, and I did them. I did them because I knew that sort of thing could be done; I'd seen my father do it, and also because I knew that was the only way to escape my father and the family. It was only later that I realized how much that trait was my father's. There are other ones that go with that. For example, I get into doing things and I get angry, I get frustrated in ways that are just like my father. I say things and have outbursts just like my father did.

My mother, who died ten years ago, was obviously the important creature in the family, especially where I was concerned. One of the interesting things as I reflect back on it is that my brother and sister see her very differently. They see her in a much less sympathetic way than I do. I think in some ways their views are probably more accurate. We were divided up: my grandmother got my brother and my father got my sister and I got my mother. That's to say when we went out on outings each adult had a child. And in some ways I think that pattern really persisted. My mother and I were very close sometimes, in some ways. I really was, in an important sense, very much in love with her in ways that I didn't know how to acknowledge. And always I was tied to her. I know that, because when she died, I was suddenly released from having to, well, partly having to conceal my sexuality, for example. Released from having to live out my life for her, in some ways. I didn't realize I was doing that until she finally died.

When we were growing up, she was very seductive to me. I mean in a physical way, sometimes. Not sexually, but very physical, like on cold mornings I'd get up and Dad of course would be gone to work, who knows where the other kids were, and she had me crawl in bed with her and she would snuggle up and stay warm. She did it with other kids, too, but not as much. She wasn't obviously playing favorites. And it was always said in my family that I was most like my mother. She was an artist, she painted and so forth, and I was the one who was charged with having artistic talent. That was a bunch of hoopla, it wasn't really true, but that's the way I think the relationship was acknowledged in the family. She was always the one that I would tell things that were important. I would tell her about them first and when she acknowledged them they were real, they were officially recorded. And she usually managed to deal with my father for me.

She was the one who always told us when we were children that we would go to college if we wanted to. They'd help us do that. So it was instilled in us very early that that was what happened after high school. She was always very liberal: do what you want, become what you want, and we'll decide when you get there. She was always the one that it was possible at all to talk with about sex, but the family was never very open. None of the family was, not to my mother, no one. And so it was not very frequent. The topic just simply didn't come up.

I'm like her in too many ways. I have the same kinds of interests that she does. She was very interested in politics and books, and reading things and talking about ideas, and so forth. My brother and sister say that I am like her. But I don't really understand what they're responding to when they say that. I think that's a myth in the family. They think that she was a lot less approachable and a lot less sympathetic to them than I thought she was. They harbor certain kinds of resentments against her.

EARLY SOCIAL EXPERIENCES

From what I can tell, when I was growing up I was very hard to turn off when I got going. I just simply never knew when something was at an end. I would just keep going on playing some game, I'd want to go on playing. If I was teasing somebody I'd go on teasing. I'd just kind of be all out. I think that led to real problems. My mother used to say that I needed a spanking about every week to sort of keep me in line and just sort of keep my equilibrium. And I think that probably was right.

I thought of myself as a sissy. I remember one time, this was a very rare occasion, one of the guys from the next block shot a BB or a slingshot at me, so I got angry at him and started yelling at him and walked away. He followed me down to my house, sort of daring me to fight. And I could have; I was stronger than he was. I'm sure I could have weathered that, but I didn't want to do that. And so I refused to fight and that was ended. But the interesting thing was my father saw it. I went in and my father went on about my being a sissy. And I felt like he'd found me out.

EARLY SEXUAL MEMORIES

I had a real problem dealing with my sexuality, which I didn't really understand at the time. I knew that I was attracted to guys and I was clear about that. I'd been clear about that for a long time. I just didn't know that that was particularly significant.

I remember, when I was about 10, sitting on the porch at my grand-mother's house, and there was a little boy there who was about the same age I was, who I had gotten to know a little bit. And we went in the garage and pulled out peepees and showed them to one another and so forth. And I asked him if he was "that way." I don't know what I meant when I said "that way," but I fully knew that there was some way to be. I was clearly interested in him and I knew that. I mean there were all these girls that I had had lots of sexual play with and I didn't really care two bits about it all. This guy was different. So I realized that was something special. I didn't know what it was. I think I was just between the eighth and the ninth grade, probably around 1951 or '52, when I finally asked my brother one time what a fairy was, or what a queer was. I wasn't sure what the words were. I think I knew, because when my brother told me I wasn't surprised, it just confirmed what it was. But I think what it did was it made it clear that there was an officially recognized category. I soon realized that that's who I was. And I remember that I went to the library to look up things on homosexuality to see what I could find. There was practically nothing in the library in this small town. The books said there's a kind of phase people go through, a homosexual phase, and they get over that. I thought possibly this will pass at some point. And that's about all the enlightenment I had. I got it from books.

As far as activities were concerned, I did some things that I didn't understand very well at the time. What happened was there was one guy that I had sexual relations with during that period. And I don't know whether he was actually gay or not. We would just go up and play with one another to orgasm. By the end of the tenth grade, we didn't do it anymore. I had become friends with a group of people who were, well—they weren't the center of the most popular group—but there were three or four of us who were interested in school, learning things. And we palled around a lot. As it turned out, I fell in love with one of them. It was a relationship that could not be acknowledged on any kind of sexual level.

I spent a couple of years being in love with him. We wrote letters, lots of letters to one another. I was still in love with him when I was about 19 or 20. I told him that summer between my sophomore and my junior year in college, about being homosexual and that I really did love him, and his response was really very bad. I was worried about keeping it a secret and his comment was, "Well, I won't tell anybody unless I have to." Suggesting that if I threatened, if I would try to make a pass at him or something like that, that he would use that as a weapon to keep me in line. When I said goodbye to him that night he said "Don't call me, I'll talk to you later." I was really broken. The last day before I went back to college he finally called. He'd gone out of the house to the airport to a pay telephone to call me to say goodbye and to ask me, "What are you going to do, what are you going to do with your life now that you're homosexual?"

In some ways I never really doubted that I was homosexual. I thought for long periods of time that I could train myself to be heterosexual, that human nature was plastic enough that it could be molded in certain ways, and all you had to do was practice and get used to it and so forth. So my sexual history for most of the time, certainly through college and graduate school, is essentially a history of having sexual relationships with women, sometimes ongoing. I was engaged a couple of times.

Sometimes women are very interesting people. Some of them were good people. But I didn't tell them about my sexual feelings and that meant that I was dealing with them essentially in a fraudulent way. I was pretending. I felt guilty about my lack of desire, lack of reciprocity of interest. It gave me an enormous amount of power and control over them because I didn't have the same kind of vulnerability they had in the relationship. Ultimately it was just simply not satisfying. I was as active as most heterosexuals would be, but I wasn't really interested in it. I remember being distinctly unsatisfied. Unsatisfied because, I remember thinking that, while physically it feels good, I like screwing women, it's nice, but I'd like a guy with me, because then I wouldn't feel so lonely. It would just be complete then, and I wouldn't be thinking about what I really want to do is go out and find somebody I'm interested in. I was aware I was gay long before I had any homosexual relationships.

In the early 1960s, when I was in graduate school, there was another student who, for several years, we used to have sex every once in a while. I wasn't in love with him. He fell in love with me. I liked him a lot, wanted to do things with him, but he thought very badly of homosexuality. The only thing that allowed him to engage in it was that it was me that he could do it with. But that finally ended and he moved away.

Several years later, around 1968 or so, there was this colleague of mine at the university who was going through real psychological problems. We used to have sex regularly. I wasn't really feeling at peace about it all. It was really a furtive thing and I really was afraid of it. I felt guilty about it. It was very, very painful. And at the same time this was all going on, not really being satisfied sexually, not having anybody that I was sexually involved with that I could be intimate with, I was nevertheless at the university very involved with lots of people, lots of students, and the whole antiwar movement. I was really just very much in love with all of them in a way. But at every point not really permitted to be intimate with them. Always that barrier which I couldn't be out of. It was very, very painful. And during that period I started drinking more, starting on Friday afternoon, drink through Friday and Saturday then try and sober up for the week and do your work for the week. It was a kind of weekly rhythm. And I had partners in this. But I realized what I was doing to myself, what it was about.

By that time, also, I smoked a little dope and that helped, because for the first time I really started figuring out what was bothering me, asking, what's really bothering you? I realized that I was gay, that I was simply not dealing with that whole aspect of my life. A year and a half before I left to come here—no, a little more than that, two years—I realized I had to leave there and I had to deal with my sexuality, come to terms with that somewhere. A risky thing because I gave up a very nice job, lots of security, tenure. I started writing a notebook at that time. And I would just simply be as honest as I could about what I was doing. Weighing the kinds of compromises I was making. The notebook allowed me to reflect on it. I could see there was simply no two ways around it. That that was what was bothering me. My first priority was to act out my being gay, whatever the cost of that was, and it could have been a very big cost. Given that I had spent all my energy up to that point making possible the career in philosophy, I recognized that it was a choice at that point that could have meant simply destroying all that. So I moved. This was around 1970, when I was about 31.

I went to bars, got to know some people. It was all very painful, though, it was not very satisfying. I had all kinds of ambivalent feelings about it. I had really lost confidence in myself as an emotional or sexual being. Partly I didn't believe that anybody would find me attractive or when I got involved in a relationship I couldn't trust it, trust myself and them.

Then when I went back to my old university I met this 19 year old who started a gay coffee house. I got to know him and basically I was just very much taken by him. I told him about my experience, that I was gay. He was one of the first people that I told I was gay. He was interested. And then the next summer I was out there again and I ran into him and at that point we did some dancing together and made love once or twice. He said he was going to take a trip later on that year, was it alright if he stopped by to see me. So he stopped. Well, the whole thing was very short. I fell in love with him. Very, very much in love. And he came out to where I lived for about a month and it was really kind of an incredible scene. It was my first love, it really was the one; first time I ever allowed myself to be sexually and romantically involved. And to live it out. It was just really overwhelming.

I went out there on spring vacation, and in summer and stayed with him that summer. I talked him into coming back with me in the fall. He wasn't the most stable of people in the first place. He was really, in his own way, a very whimsical person. Nothing like me in many ways. I didn't know what I was doing. I was simply living through the experience for the first time. Things I think I should have lived through and gotten over with when I was 19 or in adolescence sometime, but never had. I was totally bowled over by the whole experience. And desperately, desperately in love. Then I started to have trouble with my job and tenure.

I was having these fantasies, augmented by this trouble with my job and I just really drove him away. He couldn't take that, being surrounded that way and the pressure. And he was right. I mean, it was a very sick situation. He went away to San Francisco that next summer and I had been through my first romance. I managed to get some equilibrium, got involved with other people.

CURRENT SITUATION AND EXPERIENCES

I just got involved with a guy for the last eight days. I have fallen desperately in love again. So we're not lovers now but that's what may happen. I haven't been in this situation, this state, for a number of years. Four years.

I got involved about four or five years ago with a guy who is, again, about ten years younger than I am, who was basically not very intellectual, not really interested in that, but a wonderfully warm person. Just very gentle and nurturing. And I fell in love with him. We eventually started living together and I bought a house a year or so later and we lived in that house. It was really completely satisfying in some ways. Sexually and emotionally it was really very beautiful, but we didn't like to do many of the same things. He just wasn't interested in my friends at the university, he wasn't interested in talking about things. It was dissatisfying and in some ways just not very complete. So what happened was that I got involved with someone else. I started seeing a lot of this other guy, who was somewhat older than I was and a lot more mature, able to be reflective, and able to deal with me on an intellectual level. For the first time I think in my life I started discovering not only a way to think about what I was doing, what I was experiencing and how to sort it out, but also some confidence in my ability to do that. I fell very much in love with him, too. For entirely different reasons. It got to be very painful I think for all of us, all the way around. They were both honest full involvements and there was no honest way out of either of them. So I just sort of let it ride until I went off on a sabbatical in Europe. A long way away. I let it sort of simmer for a while.

As it turned out, both relationships go on, I am very close friends with both of them, and they both have their own independent lives and involvements with other people. In a way that's worked out just fine. It leaves me, however, with this character problem. I have suspicions about my ability to be involved with one person, emotionally, sexually, and intellectually. When I went off to Europe about three years ago, I was working on a book. I had lots of time and what I was going to do on my sabbatical was deal with this emotional/sexual problem of relating to people. Well, as it turned out, the book won out. I spent all the time working on this book. Not the whole time, I had a couple of relationships, but they were not the ones I wanted, I just didn't have the interest to maintain them.

I like to meet people, get to know them, talk to them, talk about issues. I like lots of intellectual challenges and involvements and I like people who play those kinds of games. I have no fear whatsoever of taking anybody on. When you look on the other side, my personal side, dealing with the individual people in a kind of close way, I become very unaggressive, become very retiring, shy, embarrassed, even. But I find myself putting off getting involved in the kind of engagements with people that would let me discover them. I just haven't had the time to do it. I haven't had enough interest to upset what I was up to. So I've been putting it off. When I worried about it, I worried about whether I was doing it because I was afraid of it or something like that. I don't think that's really right. I think as a matter of fact it's just because there's a scarcity of time. But that may be changing now.

What I really am is a philosopher. My first concern is truth. And I really am committed to understand the whole world. I spend almost all of my waking time trying to do that. And that's so much more important to me right now than anything else. It's hard to balance. I have good friends that I care a lot about, but what I'm really doing, the part of me that's really alive right now, is involved with working with issues. I think I've really discovered something very important. It's a very exciting thing. That's really where I'm at. I would like to get my sexual life, my emotional life, together too, but that seems very peripheral to me in terms of who I am.

The work part of me is the core of who I am. I could take this back in a way that might be interesting. When I was about 14, I remember one day there was some reason why I didn't want to go to school. I remember staying out in the back yard and it was just occurring to me that here I was in the situation and here I was thinking about the situation and realizing that I could choose to act different. Basically what would happen would depend on how I chose. It really depended upon what I thought now. I recognized at that point a kind of puzzling responsibility for myself. Something puzzled me about that experience. It was like I was reflecting for the first time, and I thought about that time a lot. I keep going back to it. It's a kind of beginning.

Chapter 8

Carl
Speakeasy bars and a monogamous May–December relationship

Carl is a 70 year old born in Arkansas in 1908, he's the oldest person in the study. He recalls his parents fondly and his early sexual experiences with both boys and girls. Almost engaged to be married, Carl realized he was gay in college and discovered the speakeasy bars in New York in the early 1930s. Now retired from the public relations field, he devotes a lot of his time to collecting art. His thirty-one-year monogamous relationship with his lover is the longest of anyone's in the study and all the more remarkable because of the twenty-year difference in their ages. Carl discusses how they manage their lives and how they have adapted to many changes, including alcoholism.

FAMILY MEMORIES

My father was well respected. I think he was a very kind man. I was the youngest of three children. My brother and sister were eight and nine years older than I. He would take me places on Sundays and give me quite a bit of time. I think my relationship was very good with him.

He was well educated. He was born in the United States, but my grandparents are from Germany—German-Jewish. I did have another grandparent who was born in England and one born in the United States, so they were Arkansas pioneers. They did get there in a covered wagon and were among the pioneer families.

Every Friday night we used to go to temple, which was only a block from where my grandmother lived. We kids of course would go there not so much for the services, but she'd serve food and play chess and things like that. It was a festive occasion. We also would observe the Jewish holidays. My mother was stout and I liked to eat. None of us fasted on the high holy days but my brother and father did.

I think the relationship with my father was always good. There are things that as I grew older I saw, a certain Southern bias which just existed in the South, feelings about blacks, for example. The only real antagonism that I can think of regarding my father, and I'm trying to be honest, is one time I did something and he hit me with the wrong side of a hairbrush and I resented that and remembered it for a long time afterwards, which are things you do. You don't know why you remember it, but it seemed to me like an undeserved punishment, and yet as I think about it, it really was a very minor thing, except that it happened at a time of sensitivity in my life. He was fairly strict, but I don't think in the main it was in an unreasonable way.

My mother was a very sensitive woman. Easily hurt. She was very much a dowager type, always stout, after every meal she was going to diet. She did go on certain diets such as a lot of skimmed milk, and baked potatoes, that sort of thing, and yet was always stout throughout her life.

They had a good relationship. I think we were very fortunate in that respect. That does not mean they never argued or disagreed—they seemed fairly departmentalized. She would plan trips, she would do so-and-so. They were very different in nature. He was very much an outdoors man, looked forward to the hunting season, as did my brother. They would go out to the ranch hunting. I never cared about that. My mother loved the city. She liked New York City. I guess my father would accommodate her by going there and he would come back when the hunting season opened. She liked the shops, the theaters. Neither were art-involved. But I think they were compatible. It would be hard to find two people who were more different types—one very city oriented, and the other, my father, would have never cared about leaving Arkansas if it weren't for my mother.

My mother was a nice looking, too-stout woman. I don't mean to stress the stoutness, but it was part of her personality. A stout dowager type, with large arms, which women today don't allow themselves to have. They find ways and methods or doctors, or whatever. Large breasts, as has my sister, as have I, oddly.

She was a very sensitive person. She was not an aggressive person. My father always had to make the arrangements. She would plan the trips, my father would take care of the social things. He would be the person if you went to town he would look up the relatives, he would make the plans. After he died my mother would come out here with some regularity, and it became my project then to look up all the people that she knew so that they would see her. But, in essence, she was not an aggressive woman, and friendly enough, but you had to make the advance. According to my sister, she was very sexy. I really don't have any firsthand knowledge. Far sexier than my sister was, I mean, so I believe she was a highly sexed person.

I'm a little like her in appearance and I have the coloration. The other two children and my father are blonde and she and I are brunette. I think I have an oversensitivity which doesn't show, truthfully, too much, but that's a cover-up. I like to eat, but I watch it.

I never got along well with my older brother. It wasn't open hostility, but he did things, for example, to my mother in her later years, which I resented very greatly. I can give you an example. He had an office building which adjoined one that my mother had. When she was about 80 and her mind was beginning to cloud, he put an elevator in her building and then knocked the wall through so he could use it in his building and thought that was a very funny thing to do. I felt it was dishonest. I think if he'd asked do you mind if I do it, and said we can both use it, then I think that's a different story.

I don't know if my brother knows I'm gay. I lived seven years with a boy that he knew about. What his opinion was, I don't know. He came to visit us. Outwardly he never indicated it. I think my sister has known for some time. Partially because her husband had some peculiar early alliance, and is not really gay. I think he knew. I don't think he would ever come out and say it.

EARLY SOCIAL EXPERIENCES

I was horrible at Sunday School. I don't think I was a particularly unmanageable child. I think I was fairly amenable to most things. I didn't do everything everybody told me, like eat your spinach or whatever. I was a little withdrawn as some children are and I was a little more withdrawn than I am at present, but I'm a fairly social person.

I belonged to the debating society and I was head of various things in high school, head of the school paper, and finalist in the state extemporaneous speaking, that type of thing. I don't think I was really withdrawn.

When I was sent to boys' summer camp I could never play baseball and I would hide under the tent or under someplace. I was good at photography. I was always good at swimming and I was fairly good at horseback riding, but when it came to competitive sports such as tennis or baseball or basketball, I never had any interest. I didn't play baseball or basketball—played tennis briefly and golf briefly. I don't think I was very good at them and I don't think I was good at them because I was afraid. Also, it could be—and this could be an excuse—it could be a lack of coordination.

EARLY SEXUAL MEMORIES

I think I experimented sexually when I was 11 or 12 years old with cousins and friends. I remember my introduction to sex. Neighbor's children showed me on a rubber doll how intercourse took place, and I was sure that was because they wanted me to get stuck. Also, there were boys who would come home from school and they would experiment with chickens and I remember my dowager mother would come out and five chickens flew in her face when she opened the garage door—that type of thing. As I tell you this, I think it's amusing, but at the same time I think it's what children go through who are of an experimental nature. Now, as I say, I'm not setting the norm, but I think it's what every child who—not every child, but—children who are naturally curious do find ways to find out about sex. And I don't think that my parents really sat down and told me about the facts of life.

The early experiences were mainly playing around or mutual masturbation, that type of thing. It wasn't extensive but it existed. I have always been highly sexed. I don't think until I went away to college at the age of 16 did I have any sexual experience.

I think the first homosexual experience that I had, or one of the first, was in 1924, when somebody stopped by the dormitory my freshman year. He came in the dormitory, which of course he shouldn't have done, and I don't know how it occurred—very quickly I reached ejaculation and as one does I had this terrible remorse and terrible resentment and told him that if he ever came back I would tell the authorities. He did come back and I think I was a little bit glad to see him. I'm not sure, but again, righteousness prevailed, and I think that was about one of the earliest experiences. At boys' camp I shared a bunk and there was a little messing around and things like that, but it was equally true with women. It is not that I never had gone to bed with women at all, because there was a fair amount of that also. At what point preference took place I don't know, but it was I think at a fairly early age, around 18 or 19.

I had sex to completion with women. I had almost been engaged to this girl and I realized there was something that wasn't quite right. I thought this would be the ideal mate—very charming, very attractive girl—haven't seen her for some time. But I think as I look back on it, it would have been unfair to her and to me because I am definitely homosexual. Once the decision was made there was never any doubt in my mind.

After I got out of school, I was promiscuous. I was young enough and attractive enough at that point in time. It was the era in the early '30s when you would go to Greenwich Village and go to Harlem and have no feeling of fear. I lived at first with my cousin and he is not gay, but he would drag women over and I would occasionally have sex with them. As I look back on it I took some terrible chances.

I went to either gay bars or I went to gay places and picked up people and could have and should have been hit over the head, and I was once or twice. Fortunately, I was never arrested or anything like that and, as I say, it was almost part of the times. It was the speakeasy era. They had what they called rent parties. You'd be invited for a dollar and you have all the bathtub gin you could drink. I remember taking my sister up to Harlem and we smoked what they called reefers at the time, which was really marijuana.

I had several relationships which lasted a year or two years. I also had quite a few one night stands, but the seven year relationship was rather tempestuous. The man was an enormously attractive person who came out from Arkansas. Seven years is not particularly a short period for that sort of relationship. We had one major breakup and then went back again, as happens in such things, and once it's over it's really over. I'm sort of one to believe in breaking things if you know it's over. But again, to be totally fair, it really was a very pleasant relationship and I think in the main we were very much accepted. I can't think of any rejection.

CURRENT SITUATION AND EXPERIENCES

I was 39 when I met my current lover in 1947. He was 19 or 20. He's nineteen years younger than I. Today he is 51 and I'm 70. We still live together, we still talk, we have fun. There's still sexual attraction, which I think is quite remarkable due to my age and the longevity of the affair. Naturally, there isn't exactly the same sort of glamour as there is on honeymoon night, but there's still a strong attraction. A strong emotion. As I say, I would be the last one to tell you that we don't disagree or we don't have arguments.

I think he has been totally monogamous. I think during the early part I did play a few very minor games. In the last fifteen or twenty years I have not. One reason is I don't think anybody cared that much. You set your mind a certain way, and I just don't look. Doesn't mean I don't admire, it's just that I don't look. That still doesn't mean that I haven't been into a gay bar or haven't ever been with gay people or gay parties.

There was a time when we had sex three times a night, that is over. At least once a week, sometimes twice, now. Sex doesn't have to stop at 60.

Our age difference has not been a problem. For one thing, he is a little bit older than his age, and I think, maybe I'm kidding myself, but I think

I'm a little bit younger than my age because I'm very active and very interested and very alert at this point. We both like to travel very much. I feel this. Actually, the responsibility would have to be his rather than mine because in truth, I am the one who is going to continue to age and go downhill. I feel sorry for him in a sense that I don't want him to have to take care of me—do you know what I'm saying? So far there haven't been any problems. As I say, the financial situation is good, and if anything occurred at least I could provide.

My sister accepts our relationship. We visit her, she visits us. We've gone on trips to New York together. She accepts him entirely. To be honest with you, in most cases he has been totally accepted. Now, I'm going to bring up something which I had intended not to tell you, but there's no use not to.

He has developed a drinking problem in the last few years, which is unfortunate. Now where it came from, how it came, I don't know. But that is the only rejection which has been caused and he has now fortunately gotten over it. He goes to AA and I go to Alanon. He has a pretty good hold of it. There is always a guilt that goes with that, which they tell you you shouldn't have. Anyway, I didn't cause it. It wouldn't break it up, but it is cause for concern. It was bad enough to make him lose a job. And yet he was awfully good at the job.

There's nothing in life without some problems. I don't know anybody who is honest who doesn't have some problems. Actually, in a peculiar way, I think we've pretty well overcome the situation. It's demonstrated to him that I really care and am willing to do something about it. I don't really feel that comfortable with having anybody that totally dependent upon me. I am fairly independent, or think I am. I hate that awful responsibility, and yet it's there—like anything else, you live with it.

I have a strong personality. For example, when people come in I take over. For one thing, I really am more involved. I read more books, I go to more lectures, I study more—I have more time to do it for one thing. I'm possibly the more knowledgeable mainly because I've become more involved. As a result, I realize, it's rather obnoxious of me but I do, sort of take over.

I'm in pretty good health for my age, in fact, remarkably good health. I live comfortably. I am loved and I love. I think I'm well accepted socially. The question is how to work all the things into my day, truthfully. As I say, I work for several charities, which I know is saying what a good boy I am—I don't mean to say that—at least I keep active. I could take on more. There's hardly a day when I don't either see people or they come over or I have something to do or lunch with them or whatever—other things are unimportant. It's a very good life, which most people want, but there is a recurring depression and I can't really tell you why.

There are some days when I feel more down than up. More down than usual. But I do have this—and I don't think it's terribly apparent. I keep it to myself. I don't tell many people about it, and I don't think even the party I live with knows it. He may know that I don't feel particularly cheery that day. It's stronger than it should be. I think there's been some of it all my life. I just think recently it's become—like everything happens when you grow older—I think it becomes more apparent.

I've wondered if I shouldn't see a therapist. It's very mysterious to me. Maybe because, as I say, everything is going for me. I'm not giving you a lot of bullshit: I have a very good life. I really think I'm totally—not totally, nobody is totally—accepted. But I think I'm very much accepted. I think, as I say, I live very well. I travel a lot. I don't really know quite why I feel as down as I do often.

I think, truthfully, if I had the choice, I certainly do not recommend gaiety. I think it requires a great deal of adjustment. I think it is not really a gay society, as much as a lot of people would like you to believe it is. It is obviously more recognized and more acceptable, which is fortunate. I don't think you're fooling a lot of people, and I'm not trying to. I'm not really particularly ashamed of being gay, and I will occasionally make flip remarks, sort of gay remarks in front of people who know that I am. You can tell very quickly who accepts it and who really and totally rejects it. I have enough friends that it doesn't really make that much difference. I never push myself, or as sure as hell try not to. I have been on a trip, for example, to Egypt where there was something said that some man put his arm around another and this woman said, "Oh, I thought we had enough gay people on this," or something like that. Now, I could have answered her, but that would have been superfluous. It wouldn't have changed her opinion, and I would have made it unpleasant for other people. In other words, I shut up at times when I hear things, just as I am sure a black person does, or a woman has done for years, or anybody who is a member of a minority.

Chapter 9

Danny

All-American with girlfriends, and a first date/lover

Danny is, at 33, the youngest one in the study. Born in 1945 in upstate New York, he is vice-president at an accounting firm. He has been in a relationship for nine years with the first man he ever really dated. As an all-American, class-president-type high school student, Danny had many heterosexual experiences and fantasies. But then he meets an Air Force pilot while he is a Congressional page and the confusion and "approach-avoidance" feelings of his coming-out years begin.

FAMILY MEMORIES

My father is very successful, and is getting to retire in the next couple of years. He's President of a University, a fairly studious man. He came up through the ranks teaching and then became an administrator. Easy to get along with, basically. I've never been extremely close to him, although I have been closer than most people, I guess, and certainly much more so in the last ten or fifteen years.

There never was any problem really. We didn't have any major conflicts—all kids have conflicts—but there were no major conflicts. At the same time he wasn't the one person that I would immediately confide in about problems. I can do that more readily now. I can be a little more comfortable about saying things in front of him now than I probably was ten or fifteen years ago. About all kinds of things.

My sex life is not a subject of discussion, but at the same time he knows about it, and he's comfortable with it. He's on the board of a couple of large corporations and when he comes here every other month or so he takes both me and my lover to dinner with other members of the board. I don't know whether he makes an explanation to them or not—it may not be necessary—but he feels comfortable in doing that. He certainly doesn't have any problems dealing with it.

There's never been a confrontation over it. There's never been any kind of a confrontation, which is curious. I think it's a little unusual. I never felt the need to have a confrontation. They never put up any obstacles, and when I brought my lover home for the first time, they didn't ask any questions. It was perfectly fine for *us* to talk about the things that *we* did and *our* having this and doing that. Of course they come and visit us fairly regularly. We have a house in the country and they often come up and stay on weekends, and they know that we sleep in the same room, in the same bed, and that's not a problem. So since it never created a problem, I never had to say anything. It's one of those situations where my parents can deal with sexual matters perfectly well in conversation, but it's not something they normally do, and they certainly don't talk to my married sister or married brother about what they do in bed either.

I was never close with my father. Part of that was simply because he was always very busy and was not always available. I probably was a lot closer to him than most kids are to their fathers in a lot of ways. I come from a very close family, but I would say—out of the other family members—I was less close to him than to any of the others, and it really had to do a lot, I think, with a lack of physical presence more than anything else.

He was involved with my upbringing, because my parents tended to act as a unit rather than individually. If I had done something very wrong and there was some severe punishment, it was always done in consultation with my father. But again, he was not there a lot of times and so it became more of a situation that I would find it easier to talk to my mother about things than my father. At the same time, we were a very close family—still are—but I don't think I dealt in a lot of confidences the way some kids run and tell everything. I think we tend to keep a few more things inside. A great deal of communication in our family is done on a somewhat *sub rosa* level. You tend to know exactly what's going on, but you don't spend a lot of time talking about it. Not that it can't be said, and when it's necessary, always is said. When you're not getting your point across and somebody doesn't understand, then people are able to discuss it. There are no great shouting matches in the family, even when people feel very strongly about something, because everybody—my father almost insists on everybody having a rational approach to things. You're allowed to cry if you get upset, but things rarely degenerate into screaming and yelling matches, if ever. I'm not sure they ever have done that.

Both my parents were very, very open about sex any time we came to a question. We never got a bunny in a cabbage patch or anything like that. From the time I was 5 or 6, at least, I knew exactly where babies came from and how they were made and what have you. So my father's attitude was, I guess, fairly liberal and open about all of that. His attitude toward variant kinds of sexuality was never one of condemnation or anything like that. Basically, I guess the word I would have to use is "rational" approach.

My parents have a very good marriage. Obviously they, like anybody else, have problems. Their relationship was in so many ways—is in so many ways—so close, that as a child I didn't even realize there were any problems. And, in fact, I grew up wondering how my parents had such a perfect marriage when so many of my friends had such horrible ones. My parents basically enjoyed doing the same things, they enjoyed doing them together, spend a good deal of time together when they can. I subsequently found out that there were some problems. None of them are insurmountable and obviously haven't been, and they basically have what I would characterize as a happy marriage—a good relationship.

My mother is more emotional than my father. She's quite bright but she's much less intellectual. She's probably as bright as he is but she tends to rely more on intuition and emotion than he does. I've always been very close to her. As I said, she was the one who was always at home when I was growing up, and so she was the one who, more often, I had to rely on. Strangely enough, I am probably less like her than I am my father. I would say that she certainly has tempered a lot of the way I am, but I would think in the long run I am a little more like my father (intellectually, how I reason) than I am like her.

I never really felt that there was a whole Oedipal thing with my mother and father. I'm still very close to both of them. While I was closer to my mother, I think my brother was too, and he's straight as a stick. I've thought about it but I've never come to any conclusions that I feel satisfied with, that I thought this is what caused it. To be really honest with you, I finally decided I really didn't care because I've never had any reason to try and deal with it.

My mother was always very loving. Both my parents were—you know that old adage, it hurts me more than it does you. I think, in fact, in their case it did a little bit. They didn't like to have to discipline us, but they were, I would say, as compared to my contemporaries, fairly strict about a lot of things. They were strict about the codes they imposed on us. They really felt that we had to toe the line on those, but at the same time as I was growing up I never had a curfew, I never operated under a lot of things that other people did—a very stringent set of rules. There were stringent codes of conduct and if I violated those then I was in deep trouble, but they mainly had to do with responsibility, doing what was the right thing to do, not hurting people in any way, that sort of thing—rather than don't cross the street.

I am very close, basically, with my two younger sisters and brother. I have a sister who lives here in town. I see her several times a week and she's very good friends with me and my lover. And she knows what the whole situation is. My lover had friends who came over to spend Christmas and New Year with us, a couple of guys from London, who she also knows. She was down having drinks with us last night and with two other friends from New Jersey. She's not uncomfortable with that whole situation. We're just very close as individuals.

I'm also close to my brother. He lives in the South so I don't see him that often, but he and his wife came up to spend Thanksgiving with us. We see them a number of times a year, and we have a good relationship with both of them, both him and his wife. The one problem relationship I have—and I shouldn't say a problem relationship because we get along fine, but there is a lot of tension—is with my sister just younger than I. She's married and I think the major part of the tension there is her husband, who is a closet case. He doesn't know what to do about it, and there's not any major animosity with me at all. We haven't talked about it at all. I'm just guessing. He has a strange affinity for dragging people off to drag shows.

EARLY SOCIAL EXPERIENCES

I was everybody's darling boy. I was in fact two weeks late, but it wasn't a problem delivery or anything, and as it turned out my mother delivered all of her babies late.

I was very bright and tended to be a little studious. I learned to read in kindergarten class. They had a prereading thing and in the prereading thing I learned to read on my own. I read voraciously, so I was always very smart in school. I had a checkered career in terms of athletics—there were some things I was good at and some things I was not so good at. That used to frustrate me because I was fairly used to being good at most things, and so I tended to avoid those at all cost.

I didn't ever like to be a failure or—worse almost, because I was never really a failure (knock wood) at anything—I have a thing about not wanting to be mediocre. And I got along well with other kids. I was usually pretty popular. I was the sort of kid who got elected president of the grade school class and that sort of thing. Part of that really had to do with classroom performance more than anything else. Kids tend to look up to other kids who they think are smart. In my case it wasn't just a matter of being smart, it had to do with reading habits as much as anything else, and exposure at home as well.

I had a close friend then. I sometimes wonder about him to be honest with you. I saw him about seven or eight years ago and he was still unmarried at that point, which isn't that unusual. He was 25 or 26. But he didn't seem to be all that interested in girls. He's not in the least bit effeminate, and I would have no other reason to suspect at all. I really have lost track of him subsequent to that.

In high school, I still was the kid who was president of the class and I still was pretty bright. At that point I was playing football well, so I seemed to be an "all around" kid. I think there are some things there that I should have tweaked onto about my own sexuality, but I didn't. I really was remarkably slow in figuring out a lot of things. I don't suppose that my relationships with girls were any more tenuous than my peers, in fact I'm sure they weren't. I was unsure of myself and what have you. I resolved a lot of that fairly early on.

EARLY SEXUAL MEMORIES

I guess it was around 1960, when I was 15, that I first had sex with a girl, and I'd had a reasonable amount of experience before that—"everything but" kind of thing. And the first time I can remember having an erection was when I was 11. The occasion was trying on my first jock strap—I suppose that should have told me but it really didn't—and subsequent to that I began to have masturbatory fantasies which really were then, I think, all heterosexual, at least I never had any inkling that they weren't. I didn't necessarily identify more with a woman or anything else.

I guess when I was 12 or 13, we started having parties with boys and girls. Soon after that I was holding hands and kissing and all that sort of thing. A few years later, there was a girl who was my age, around 14 or 15. She made it abundantly clear that she would like to mess around with me—she wasn't anybody I liked but I just wanted to have sex and I did. I don't think it was her first time at all, but at the same time I didn't really feel as if I was being seduced. I somehow felt that I was being the seducer, in that respect I'm sure I was. And all of that went very well. I didn't have any real sexual problems. In fact, my only concern in growing up at that point was that I was oversexed and I suppose I am more highly sexed than a great many people are. I no longer worry about being oversexed—I'm not sure what that is anyway, but then I really thought I was. First of all because I never spent a lot of time talking with my friends about how often they masturbated or whatever, and I know I felt a little bit guilty about spending as much time as I did thinking about sex.

I generally thought about girls—at that point. The content was mainly about big breasts—that is what I eroticized at that point in my life—this again is in the early '60s, the 15/16/17 year old age. I used to talk to lots of people about circle jerks and things like that, but I never experienced one and never had one, and I don't know why. I was offered the opportunity I guess when I was 17. It was really just a mutual masturbation thing, and it was a guy that I think in retrospect I probably found attractive. I don't know whether it was latent fear that kept me from it or what it was, but he and I were sharing a cabin. We were working, lumbering up in the mountains for the summer, and we were obviously without contact all week long with women. The proposition was made on that basis: there's nothing up here so we might as well. And I said no, I really didn't want to.

About the time I went off to college, my attitude toward women changed somewhat in that I really became less interested in breasts and more interested in really shapely bodies and pretty legs, all that sort of thing, and I also began for the first time to combine sex and love thoughts, because before that I never really did. I used to date a lot of different girls but I never went steady with any one. There was only one girl I really wanted to have an emotional attachment to and at that point she wasn't interested. Subsequently she did get interested and I saw a lot of her in college—still see her. That is to say, my friend and I see her, and she's a friend of ours now, and she's somebody I practically lived with for a year and a half. That's been an interesting transition too.

Sex was fulfilling and I enjoyed it. It's not as fulfilling as what I subsequently learned about later. An orgasm is an orgasm—any orgasm is at least tension releasing if nothing else, and I really didn't necessarily think there was anything other than that. I had no reason to think there was anything better out there.

To show you how naive I was—at 16 I was a page for Congress. There was a guy who was the son of friends of my parents who was considerably older than I was. He must have just gotten out of college—somebody that I knew but never been friendly with. I used to see him on a social basis with my parents and his parents. One day out of the blue he called me up in Washington, long distance. He said he was coming to Washington, just gotten out of college, and he was doing pilot training in the Air Force. He said he had finished all this training and all he had to do was log out. He was thinking of coming to Washington that weekend and knew I was there and would I be around and could I show him the sights.

I was very impressed. I wasn't used to guys that age paying attention to me. I thought that was a big deal. So I spent the day with him on Saturday, took him all around. Showed him the back doors of the Capitol, and then he was going to take me out to dinner at Andrews Air Force Base, which was where he'd come in, at the Officers' Club. So he said we'd need to change into a suit and tie. I took him back to my apartment and he watched while I undressed and took my shower and got all dressed up. We went out to Andrews Air Force Base, then we went to where he was staying so he could shower and change into his uniform. He said, "Don't you want to take a shower?", and I was thinking, he just saw me do that 45 minutes ago. I said, "Oh, no thank you." So he gets all undressed and says, "You sure, they have great showers here." And I said, "No, really, I'm not interested in another shower." He got in the shower and a little while later he sticks his head in the door and said, "Come on in, it really feels good." At this point I was smelling my armpits, and thinking I must be offensive or something, I couldn't figure out what was going on. He finally gave up on the shower ploy and took me to dinner.

I remember how impressed I was when he ordered wine with dinner. I was very impressed that he was getting wine for me, since I was only around 16. He plied me. He poured most of it in my glass. I guess, fortunately, I have a hollow leg—so it didn't phase me at all. But after dinner we went back to his place to watch television and we're sitting there. He takes off all of his clothes except his underpants and he's sitting there saying "Isn't it warm, don't you want to get undressed?" and I was very comfortable. I said, "No, thank you and besides I've got to go back," and so on and so forth.

Along about midnight, the last bus back into Washington came and I said I've got to go. He got furious with me. He did this whole number because he'd obviously wasted his whole day and got nowhere. And I literally didn't tweak onto any of this. For years it bothered me because I couldn't figure out why this guy got so angry with me. I thought I'd said something wrong and he, subsequently, mind you, has gotten married, has several children. I don't know if he ever does anything or not. I was probably 25 before I knew what had happened nine, ten years earlier.

Anyway, that sort of shows you where my mind was. Several other things like that happened to me that only in retrospect did I realize that people were making a play. They obviously saw something that I didn't know about yet. I didn't have any kind of homosexual experience until I was in college and then—I guess there were four or five—always somebody else made the advance and it was strictly a "hands behind the head blow-job" for me. I'm not involved, and if it feels good, who cares. I never sought one out. I guess there were really only three, one was a repeat—glee club director. And another one was with the guy upstairs who I'd gone to a mixer with. We came back and the next morning he did the "oh boy, was I drunk" thing and I just told him I didn't remember anything. And the last one was somebody who was very serious about it and wanted to repeat. In the meantime I had a very active heterosexual sex life, with a number of different girls, but primarily with that girl that I mentioned earlier, the one that I'd been interested in since high school.

When I got out of college in 1967, I was about 22, and when I came to New York, I began to have some gay fantasies. I worked for a bank down South for about seven or eight months right out of college and I decided I didn't like being a big fish in a small pond and I wanted to come to New York. While I was in the South I began to have an occasional fantasy that—I'm not sure then I realized—was about men. It was a fantasy that involved heterosexual sex, but it centered much more on blow-jobs, which I've never really gotten women to do, either well, or be willing to do in general.

I met a guy who was in law school at the time. He was a classmate with some guys I went to college with. And there began a very strange relationship that lasted a little over a year. He was gay. I'm not sure in the beginning I knew he was gay. He made a big pretense. We double-dated and did that sort of thing, but we also just went out together. He was very interested in the theater and dancing and knew a lot of people and got all kinds of tickets. He'd call me up and say let's go to this and do that and so on and so forth, but still nothing ever passed between us. I met a lot of his friends, a lot of people he knew were in the theater or dancers, who were very open about being gay. At first I was a little uncomfortable, then I thought this is very nice. Isn't it nice to be able to know these people. When I say "uncomfortable" I just always felt I wasn't sure how I was supposed to act and I was afraid of saying the wrong thing or doing the wrong thing. And as time progressed I got to feel very comfortable and friendly with them, in fact even had a couple of experiences—unbeknownst to my friend—but, more "hands behind the head" kind of thing. Not more than three or four maybe.

So no word ever passed between us, but I began to realize that he was gay. Still all the time double-dating and what have you. We got to be very, very good friends and he was always doing things for me. In retrospect it was a little bit sick, and when I realized what I realized I should have said something to him about it, because I just played it, I didn't do anything about it. He was not somebody I wanted to go to bed with. He wasn't unattractive but he wasn't at that point to me any way physically attractive. I wasn't at all interested in going to bed with him.

During that time I began to think more and more about what men did in bed together, with both partners being active as opposed to passive situations, which was all that I had experienced. And I thought about it and thought I would really like to try it, but I also didn't have enough nerve. I was also sort of waiting for the right person too, I think, in a lot of ways. So, this continued for a year until I went back to graduate school. I would still come down on the odd weekend and see this guy, stay with him in his apartment, and still nothing ever happened—nobody dropping a hairpin. It was just all very buddy kind of thing.

About halfway through my first year in graduate school I got a call from a big bank in Boston. They had read my resume and a series of things I had done in the bank and it turned out that I seemed to fit into a slot with a specific project being done the next summer and they called me and said, "Would you be interested in coming in for an interview?" So I said sure, 'cause I was looking for a summer job. I went in for the interview and met this guy who was very nice and got along famously, so a couple of days later he called me and said he was very impressed. He said, "Would you consider coming in to have dinner with my boss and me this weekend?" I said that would be very nice. We went to a nice restaurant and then his boss said he lived in the suburbs somewhere. He needed to catch a train and he was going to go back and he said, "I'll leave you two bachelors to...", you know, that kind of bullshit. And after he left I said, "Where do you want to go?" and he said, "Well, do you like kinky bars?"

At this point I'd been to several gay bars with several gay friends, and the first couple had made me uncomfortable. After that I didn't mind, except I did get a little annoyed when people would try to put the make on you, because I still thought I didn't want that. But he said, "What about a kinky bar?" and I sort of felt that was what he meant, but I didn't know. So I said fine. And he took me to a bar which was not strictly gay but it was mostly gay. He said, without saying anything about himself, "There are a lot of gay people here but this is a nice bar and do you mind?" And I said no. So we had a couple of drinks and that was it. And he said, "You know I'll probably want to make you an offer."

So a week or so later he called me up—didn't say anything about the offer, but he said, "I feel like going out and having a drink tonight, what are you doing?" I said studying, and he said, "Can you get away for an hour?" and I said yes, and he said, "Let's meet at the same bar." And we went there and then he said, "There's another bar right down the street, around the corner actually," and we went there and that was a strictly gay bar—very cruisey. He said, "Does it bother you?" and I said, "No that's fine." And we had some drinks and I had to get back and get to work. So he called me again in another week.

We were meant to meet at the very same gay bar, and I got there and waited an hour and he wasn't there. That made me a little nervous because it was the first time I'd been all by myself. When I got in, the bartender motioned me over and he said, "Your name's Danny, isn't it?", and I thought, "Oh Jesus, now I'm in trouble." And he said, "So-and-so just called and he's delayed but please wait for him here, he'll be here shortly."

So I got myself a drink and sort of stood up against the wall and there was this guy on the other side of the room that I felt was very attractive, who was trying to make eye contact with me. I was just looking away and kept looking at my watch, trying to appear as if I weren't interested and this whole game went on for a half hour or so while I was waiting for this guy. Meanwhile, the guy who was making eye contact moved around the bar closer and closer and finally he walked up and said, "Hi, how are you?" or something innocuous. We had this—"do you come here often", "no, I'm just meeting a friend"—one of those conversations.

Just about that time the guy I was meeting came in. End of conversation. I went over to the bar and had a drink with this guy, and I'm still not sure how I managed to screw up enough courage to do it, but after a drink the guy said, "Let's go to another bar," and I said, "No, I think I'll stay here," and he was very surprised. I said, "I'm just gonna stay, you go on though and have a good time," and that sort of left him no option. So he left. And I resumed eye contact with this other guy and he came over and started talking to me again. As it turned out, it was all very bizarre because we both knew a number of straight people in common through other people. And he said, "Would you like to come back to my apartment for a drink?" and I knew perfectly well what he meant and I just decided this was going to be it, and it was.

Again, I didn't do anything other than jerk him off that night, but I kissed him and I'd never done that before—that was a major mission—and I liked it and I was very excited by it. I was a good deal more excited by it than I was afraid of it—I was very afraid of it too. But I was very excited and I did two strange things, which I guess will show you the dichotomy of my mind at that moment. I agreed to meet him the next Tuesday night at his apartment for dinner, which was already an admission, but at the same time, the next morning early, I called up this girl in New York and said, "Look, I'm coming in for the weekend, are you free?" and I screwed like crazy all weekend long. Sort of a re-affirmation that I'm really not like that—ha ha—at the same time I wasn't ready to break the date on Tuesday. What we agreed was that we would reconfirm that one of us would call the other at six—and right on the stroke of six I dialed his number and it was busy. We both did that for five minutes. We were dialing each other's number. And he's the same person I'm still living with nine years later, which I think is somewhat unusual anyway.

I still went through an approach-avoidance, avoidance-approach all the rest of the half of that year: whether that was really what I wanted and whether I was really that way. I made a number of excursions to go to bed with girls to make sure I wasn't losing that. I knew every time I went out with a woman it was to reaffirm my masculinity—I knew that—but at the same time I couldn't not do it. It was one of those things—because I felt stupid sometimes doing it, but at the same time it really wasn't as clearcut as that. When I'd go to bed with a guy I would think that this isn't really what I thought it was, and it really is better with women and where will this lead. Homosexuals have terrible lives, and wouldn't it be nice to have a wife and a family and home and all that sort of stuff.

But there's no question that I'm gay. I have been, as far as I'm concerned, ever since the first year. Once I sorted it all out and knew that I liked this better; and while I don't think I'd have any problem going back to women, I just don't have any desire to do it.

I didn't feel comforted by it at first. I knew that I loved it and that I particularly loved this guy in a way that I'd never loved any woman. And that grew over time, it did not get less. Finally, I could breathe a sigh of relief and do what I really wanted to do all along. Here's something that I really like that I didn't know about before. Other people have told me it was wrong or it was going to be difficult or problematic. Do I really like it enough to sacrifice everything? Do I really want to make this kind of decision, or do I have to make this kind of decision? I played both ends against the middle. Can I be bisexual? What is that? In a lot of ways it was a matter of sorting out.

CURRENT SITUATION AND EXPERIENCES

In the broadest sense of the word, we have been monogamous, but there have been a couple of excursions. Only on my part, I think, not on his, although he would probably tell you that same thing. Part of that in my case was simple curiosity. When you suddenly have a relationship with the only man you've ever really had an active sexual relationship with, you wonder what else is out there. The other thing, as I said, is I'm fairly highly sexed and in occasional lapses when he's a little less interested, then I'll do it, but it happens very infrequently. It's never been a situation of another relationship or even a multi-occasion affair.

The bad parts are the tensions of constantly making it work. It's not always easy; you don't always get to take the easiest course out; you don't always do everything you want to do. Everything doesn't always go your way. Really, that's it. The bad parts are only just the hard work involved in making a relationship, as far as I'm concerned.

The good parts I could go on about for a long time. The good parts are having a bigger life and sharing it with someone. The good parts are mutual support and interdependence. The good parts are doing lots of things with someone, sharing them. In a lot of ways I suppose we're closer than our friends. I think we're a little peculiar in that way in that we probably have a greater percentage of friends in a long-term relationship than most people do. The good things are just a real feeling of happiness. We're both very pleased with where we are and where we're going.

We have a house up in the country. We go up there on the weekends. During the week, when we're in town, we see friends. We have a number of straight friends as well and we see them. But we go to the theater, we go to the opera—and then when we get to the country we see a lot of people up there. We both like to cook a lot so we like to entertain. We also do projects all the time—build things and what have you.

I'm not at all open at work, with one exception. My current boss knows that I am because as it turns out, he is too. I had suspicions but I wouldn't have come out to him necessarily but he did to me. I admire him for that. At the job that I had just before this one, I discovered after I'd gotten there that my predecessor had been fired. Everybody was talking that he was fired for that reason. That is a little discomforting if you yourself are. And particularly since in my personal life I don't make any pretense. It is very easy if someone wants to find out and make an issue of it. I later found out that that probably wasn't the real reason he got fired, he got fired because he was incompetent.

I do go to church. I'm certainly not there every Sunday. I go mainly on festive occasions, if you want to call it that. In a lot of ways I suppose I am very religious. I do pray privately, regularly. I am a little uncomfortable in organized religion. I was confirmed in the Episcopal Church, but I could not honestly affirm the creed. For instance, I would find it dishonest to say that I believed in the Trinity, nor could I affirm the virgin birth, necessarily. That makes me a pretty bad Episcopalian, which is another reason why I'm not a regular churchgoer.

If there is a business party and people are expected to bring a date or a wife, then I do bring a date. It's generally awkward not to, uneven number at the table and that sort of thing, but so far as making up stories to tell people—this is the girl I'm going steady with—I never do that. I don't want not to be gay.

Chapter 10

Ed
Immigrant, late bloomer, and independently single

Ed is 44 and has been living in this country for almost twenty years. He
was born in Norway in 1935 and currently teaches mathematics at a
university. He is not involved in a relationship at this time. Ed talks
about his Norwegian character and how this may have influenced his
feelings about relationships. He sees himself as fiercely independent
and self-sufficient, a theme that recurs throughout his experiences. Ed
did not come out until the 1960s, having been a late bloomer sexually
because, he feels, of his "puritan religious" upbringing.

FAMILY MEMORIES

My father was a very successful professional, writing a local newspaper—
publisher, editor. Fairly intellectual although he did not have a university
degree—that was not terribly common when he grew up. Fairly conservative in outlook, though maybe a little bit of an old-fashioned moralist.
Active in politics. Pretty much involved in his job. Not so interested in
the family. Preoccupied with his newspaper—certain politics mainly, and
providing for things in the family, sure—making the big decisions but not
taking much interest in details of how the home was run. That was left to
my mother. Taking some interest in my school—he was very keen on
education and so on—not so interested in my psychology or my own
personal sense of happiness.

He maintained a fair amount of distance. Not quite austere, but a little
remote. I would not talk to him about any sort of intimate problem. I was
a little scared. He would scold me. He would talk to me sternly. He never
hit me or anything. I sensed he favored me over my older brother.

My parents probably had a cold marriage. Everything was kept very
private—away from kids—an old-fashioned, rather puritan attitude probably. They very, very rarely kissed each other. Nobody kissed. It's not

done. I think it's terribly much a Scandinavian tradition; touching and kissing might be an Italian tradition. My family was probably cooler than average. Cool environment.

I would say their marriage was a below average success, and I pressed my mother a little bit once after my father died and she did admit that they weren't just right for each other, but that's as intimate or detailed as she would get.

I am like my father in some intellectual interests. He would enjoy subjects like law or economics, the way I do too. So in that sense, intellectually, we might be slightly similar. He was keen on languages—grammar, reading—sort of bookish interests that we would share. I don't share his old-fashioned attitudes. Whether that's a generational gap or personality difference is hard to say. But in my lifestyle I'm very different.

I was very surprised when my father died. I didn't expect it at all. I was 14. Everybody thought you'd get through a little operation. I can't really say it was a big personal loss. He was remote and, when I thought it over later, he didn't mean a lot to me. I was more scared of what was going to happen to the family. My mother told me it might mean a lot of sacrifices, lower income, and so on, but she started to work and it wasn't so bad—it was no big personal loss. Maybe I was a little offended by the fact that my mother did not seem terribly upset by it either, after a while, so I was a little puzzled by the coolness about it, and was distraught by the fact that my father's name was hardly ever, ever mentioned afterwards. It was a sign of a bad or unsatisfying family setup to begin with.

My mother is bright—a bit superficial—she's maybe as bright or brighter than my father was, except she does not have the intellectual inclination. She doesn't pursue any abstract problems. She's quick—quick at making judgments too, and now I can sense that she's fairly frustrated, a rather bitter woman. I didn't quite realize it as a child. The way I size her up now is that she probably had a not terribly good childhood herself and she's retained a certain bitterness against her own parents. She was very negative, like her parents, her family. She's carried with her some bitterness, vindictiveness, maybe against men even. She never seemed to like her father. She never seemed to like her husband. And so I sensed that anti-male quality in her, not terribly powerful, but a certain bitchiness.

She did not marry again. She went back to work after my father died and that gave her something to do and she probably had a bit of a second bloom in her 40s. When my father was dead she started to live a professional life of her own, made friends and she seemed very happy then. A couple of times I noticed she had guys around who she was dating a little bit. I don't know how far that went at all. Now of course she's retired and probably just sitting at home and mulling over her life or her bitterness. In that sense she's not a terribly happy woman.

I guess I was fairly distant from her too when I was young. She was distant from me. Even though she was around all the time we did not have close human communication. I probably didn't sense that she really was terribly interested in my personal inner feelings. She took care of me; she was a good mother in a superficial sense. But looking back now on a psychological frame, I don't think either one of my parents was terribly helpful, constructive.

She probably was a bit closer to my brother. She favored him. My father favored me. Awkward cleavage in the family. I used to write to my mother once in a while. I haven't written for over a year. Our relations did not improve the last time I was home, probably got a little worse. My mother had relapsed into a bitter, vindictive attitude that I thought we would have gotten over, complaining bitterly about my habits or my staying out too late, getting very upset about trivial things and not caring to reconcile before I left. So she declared my visit a failure and I guess I took that as a firmer step away from my family.

My brother is six years older—a little too much for us to be good playmates. We had a rather, well, competitive relationship as children and that did not really make us good friends. We didn't grow up as friends— we were too far apart in age to. Competition within the family made it worse than it needed to be. I suppose we've retained that. He's probably trying to be friendly now if he ever sees me, but it's so rare—there's no occasion for that—he still lives in Norway. We never had any sort of, shall I say, reconciliation as grownups. We didn't go on fighting after we grew up, but still retained some sort of remoteness.

EARLY SOCIAL EXPERIENCES

My older brother used to say that I cried a lot when I was very little, just after I was born. I don't know if that was something he invented for competitive purposes or whether that's true. Otherwise, I was probably healthy, fairly normal, well-behaved baby as far as anybody could tell. Always did very well in school. Was generally healthy. People would say I looked good, pretty baby, good-looking kid, smart kid, well-behaved—a little on the shy side as I grew up. I was probably shyer than average, a bit more withdrawn or reserved than the average kid, perhaps less prone to get involved in a lot of games. A bit more bookish for one thing—a bit more intellectual and less prone to take part in ball games or riding around with kids.

I wasn't especially bad in athletics but I was awkward in a sense of being shy and self-conscious, I suspect more than most kids. Not interested in soccer for instance. Soccer is the big game there—football, basketball, baseball—not terribly keen on that. Not terribly interested in skiing and things that the majority of kids care for. I resented pressure from school and family that I engage in that, so that was a little bit of a sore psychological friction for me. I was at least average in gym class, so I probably was weak on the active sports side, but I was still a fairly healthy, normal child in most other respects.

I knew I wasn't as active physically, playing around as much as other kids. I suspect that that gave me a little bit of feeling like a sissy. I don't think I felt girlish. I felt awkward, gauche, or shy, and felt pressured about that. People didn't really call me sissy. People probably respected me for other reasons—doing well scholastically makes a bigger difference in that society than it does in American society, so still I had an acceptable social standing. A little weak on the sports side but otherwise a good or even admirable kid. My father might have scolded me a couple of times for not being active enough or relatives asking, "Aren't you gonna play soccer?" or something like that—I felt this pressure and that bothered me, so, it's a little bit of that feeling.

I suspect where we lived then, there were more girls than guys. I played around—living in a suburban residential area—in the gardens, hide and seek games. There were a couple of girls I was very friendly with and probably even kidded about, kids go together even at such an absurdly early age. So a couple of the neighborhood people I would be considered fairly close to, and some of them I would know ten years later and others would fade out.

And then in my teens, I went to an all-boys school. I obviously had more male friends when I went to school, a few of them were close buddies of mine. I probably tended to have a smaller circle of friends than most people, and I would have one or two good friends—perhaps for years, and these kids would probably be among the more intellectual kids at school. Kids who also did not particularly care about sports and probably had sort of an arrogant attitude toward people who did like sports, people who did not share our intellectual interests. We were arrogant intellectually, perhaps in self-defense.

EARLY SEXUAL MEMORIES

Thinking back, puberty was a bit rough. I was confused, naive and ignorant about sexual matters, and I guess I didn't understand bodily changes. My parents gave me no guidance—no psychological support. They hardly have in any respect in my life—that's what I'm saying. Materially, they gave me good support. Nobody talked. Of course, at the time, school did not give any guidance or any psychological help to a kid growing up. Perhaps now it's changed. Perhaps now they have sex education; we did not. So I was probably behind in terms of—let's call it "sexual psychological development." I understood less of my own adolescence than some of my rougher, less intellectual friends. So I was probably confused about it and didn't understand it. I don't recall any particular traumas either. It was a tense period—I sometimes slept poorly. Probably found strange rationalizations for my awakening sexual feelings, fantasies, or sublimations.

I matured quite late in sexual terms. There's a cute illustration that amuses almost everybody, especially people who have any superficial knowledge of the sexual freedom in Scandinavia. I never even masturbated. When I first heard about this, I read magazine articles and at that time apparently public opinion was just changing so that masturbation was no longer considered unhealthy or harmful. I remember reading about this—not understanding what this was all about. So I had a peculiar, naive, or even prudish attitude towards sex, including masturbation. Only crazy people would do a thing like that. And probably I've gotten some of this, well almost, prissy, puritan attitude through partly a puritan religious heritage, schooling and all that, partly through my family's refusal to deal with sexual matters in an open, frank way. So, I never had sex either in my teens.

I thought of sex in terms of hygiene. You don't want to have anything to do with genitals. They're dirty. Use your cock for pissing and that's it. So I was negative on sexual matters on many different levels—somewhat repelled, repulsed by the thought of sex organs and of male and female genitals—and that's difficult for me to get over. And I didn't even masturbate—not until I'd had sex with other people. Most of my friends find it highly peculiar that somebody has had voluntary sex for the first time at 23½ and that was 1959, the year I moved to the States.

I met people there and started to loosen up after that and gradually made it a practice, so probably a year later I was moderately active. Not terribly active, but still moderately active, even though I must have retained some of my childhood reservations. I had difficulty feeling natural about it, difficulty really enjoying it, or having very mixed feelings about physical pleasure coupled with psychological anxieties. The first thing that ever happened sexually was that a not so good friend of mine more or less seduced me when I was 18 while I was in the Navy. And I was surprised and confused and angered—it happened so fast. I didn't understand what was going on—embarrassing to say that at that age I did not—and I was annoyed and confused about that. I wouldn't have anything to do with sex for years. And did not loosen up until I was about 23.

I spent a couple of summers during the late 1950s in the French Riviera when I was still living in Norway. I'd go down there ostensibly to study French, but meeting people, having a good time. A lot of things were going on there—a lot of gay people, especially in Cannes. Meeting some of them, hanging out with them—then I realized that socially I had a better time with the gay crowd. I mean, they were much more receptive to me than most straight people, so suddenly I found myself more popular than I'd ever been, even though I didn't know how to cope with sexual matters as they came up. Gradually I allowed myself to experiment and I started to have a little sex. I was just moving to the United States the same year or the following year at 23.

It was difficult thinking that I might be a true homosexual. I probably tried to rationalize it away, or just was very confused about it. After a few years I guess I was honest enough to cope with that, and I knew that I had not so strong feelings for women. As a teenager I remember being physically turned on by some girls, but that probably stopped happening gradually in my early 20s—as I got more oriented to men. Sometimes I've thought that heterosexual sex would be a thing for everybody to try and go through. Intellectually, perhaps one should try everything. But have I had the physical urge? I'd say no.

The first year or two I was out, I only allowed myself to be picked up and I was very passive in that respect. I thought of myself as an object more than a subject. In that respect I felt secure, that way I didn't have to risk my own ego. At the same time I probably got a little bit attached to some people, or was impressed with them and felt I had strong feelings for some of them. Certainly, if I wanted to see people over and over again, I would have to take some action to do that. I had to be a little bit more active.

Probably a couple of years after this I had my first long-term friend. Maybe around 1961 or '62, just two years after I came out. I saw him for a half a year regularly. I was back in Norway for a while, so I had my first affair of any length. I've probably stuck with the same pattern since then. Being single, pretty much on my own. Going out with the idea of meeting people. Not being terribly active—becoming a little more active socially, seeking people out a little bit more, but still most of the time allowing other people to approach me. Occasionally having affairs that last more than weeks.

Once in San Francisco I had a close friend, more or less a lover, that lasted for three years. Then I moved to the East Coast and we probably were breaking up anyhow. The last ten to thirteen years I would say I have not had anything like a permanent lover. I've had affairs that might have lasted up to two months—and of course a lot of shorter things between that.

CURRENT SITUATION AND EXPERIENCES

Like other people, I want to have it both ways always—freedom and permanence and attachment and everything at the same time—which is not quite possible. Logically contradictory or impracticably possible. So I'm fairly happy with that, except if you pose it this way: I suppose in theory if a perfect lover came along that would be even better; so I sometimes hold out that possibility. Not terribly realistic, but I want to be ready for it if it were to happen—I don't want to close that.

Maybe I'm not looking for anything defined enough, and maybe there is nothing that could exist that I'm looking for. I'm not sure what it would be, but obviously I want somebody who is intellectually stimulating—I have to talk to people. I can hardly sustain any physical interest in people if they're not also socially, personally, intellectually worthwhile. Probably I want someone who is not terribly into the overt gay scene. I'm fairly, you might even say conservative, in my own lifestyle. I'm not flamboyant. I don't carry on in public. I don't particularly like my friends to do it either—maybe partly out of my own social insecurity. Obviously I've maintained a bit of a schizophrenic life—my professional life being quite straight and conventional on the surface and my private life being quite different. If I had a close friend he would have to respect that duality in my situation, and probably he would have the same one too. I would prefer a person who has a good professional life himself—because that means a lot to a person—his interests, his ego, and that probably would give him the chance to use his mind too, and that probably would make a relationship more satisfactory for the parties. So if somebody like that came around—a smart, attractive guy who shares my attitude towards lifestyle and some other things—possibly, possibly.

I keep my colleagues separate, socially. The only thing that would happen is that somebody on the faculty in the department would have a party once or twice a year and of course I attend. My chairman has a party I go to. Once in a while there will be somebody who suggests that we go out. Somebody actually asked me two weeks ago: "Since you know the city so well, why don't you show me around some day." A straight guy who wants to get away from his wife. I don't care to do that. I don't think I have to. If somebody says, "Let's go out and have a drink, and we might even talk about school matters," I guess I would say OK. I would actually prefer not to. And being a teacher in a large city, it's easier to get away with that. If I had a job in the Midwest, in a small-town college, I would probably be expected to participate more on a social level, and there would be more questions raised about what I'm doing and watch my style, why don't I have a wife. Here hardly anybody seems to care. If they do they don't say anything.

I think I've maintained the same social pattern for the last fifteen years probably. Going out a little bit, meeting people a little bit, not being hyperactive. On average, if you ask me to pull together some statistics, I meet a new person every two weeks, perhaps. Most typically in a bar situation. I do go to the gay bars. Occasionally go to parties, meet people in that way. Seeing somebody sometimes only for one evening. Occasionally for several dates after that, but most of the time of course not on a prolonged basis. Once in a while it happens that we become friends afterwards. Perhaps sex once or twice and then become social friends— that does happen in a minority of cases. So, I'm moderately active at the bars. I never got into the baths. They never interested me, although somebody must have taken me along once or twice, but that's not my scene. Occasionally I meet people on the street if the social situation is just natural. I wouldn't go out and look for people on the street—it's not practical or terribly productive—but I would enjoy meeting people in unexpected social circumstances. In the restaurants or on the street, wherever, I don't mind striking up a conversation with strangers if they seem pleasant and approachable, or I let them approach me, perhaps, more typically.

I go out to dinner, go to the theater, go to the movies, occasionally go to bars with other people, so probably you would say I have, well, a fairly large group of friends or social acquaintances. Some of us go out either two of us, or a small group, and I need that—I enjoy that. And we share some of the same gay interests. In most cases we do not have sex now, we probably have had in the past. In a few cases we might have an occasional sex scene, nevertheless.

Philosophically, I think that if a life's miserable perhaps it should be ended. I have no religious qualms about suicide. So that if my life turned very bad I should consider it and I hope I would have the strength to terminate my life if it was that bad. I have thought of suicide, but more as a child. I suspect it's part of my heritage to think about it and half plan it, but not doing it. You may know that it's a bigger feature of my culture. As a child I probably thought of actually doing it, and I even made one or two fake attempts. I look around my family, my extended family, I think there have been at latest count six suicides, so it's a common cause of death. For short, very short periods of time, I might think that way, even now, but I know that I sort of get out of that feeling usually. If I got a deadly disease or my life really turned disastrous, certainly I would entertain it.

I've thought a little bit about therapy, but not much. I've had many friends who have been in analysis and they've told me a little about it. Some of them found it very helpful, a few others thought it was a waste. Nobody could really tell me whether I would need it or benefit from it. So I've sort of rejected the idea—partly because I don't have any immediate pressing problems. I don't mean I'm free of a lot of tensions, but I function—I seem to function—and I believe I'm introspective enough to think about whatever problems I do have. In my own estimation, I solve most of them, or if I don't solve them at least I cope with them or push them aside so they don't fuck up my everyday existence.

I usually don't have any emotional outbursts either, although it might have been good for me occasionally. I tend to repress most of my feelings if I sense they would not be socially attractive—maybe a little too much. Historically I have probably repressed too many feelings. Maybe I've opened up a little bit, so it's easier to me now to let it out if I have to, but I usually feel if I have a big personal problem—stress situation, whatever—I'll have to deal with myself and not let it come out too much. It shouldn't be inflicted on other people. I don't want to lose my cool. I guess I like a fairly cool, together image and I have to resolve it myself. It may take a while and I might retain some bitterness or negative feelings afterwards—I occasionally do, but it's not a terribly big problem. I may go through a couple of bad days, I may get drunk, I may tell my best friend about it. As I do that, I'm aware of my need for that kind of outlet, so it's like I'm doing this as a form of therapy for myself.

The easiest explanation for my homosexuality is to blame my mother, of course. My mother clearly has turned me off as a personality, but my father did too, up to a point—except he faded out of the picture. He was not as present when he lived and he died when I was 14, so neither one of my parents had any qualities that made me interested in sex or feel warm toward either type of a grownup situation, so—that's very confusing. I did not have an overbearing, strong protective mother, so I don't fit in that category. Some of my friends who have discussed it with me put a different perspective on it. My mother may still have scared me out of early, easy heterosexual relationships through her relatively negative attitude toward me. She had a bitchy, vindictive quality, I sense, toward my father, toward men in general. I always had to hear how awful men were. I sense now that my mother felt that men were sexually repulsive almost. She's a heterosexual woman, but still had peculiar negative feelings about the physical aspect of men. I don't quite understand it.

Now, my father did not give me any positives about women either, so whatever the reason I do not know, it's possible that the image I have of my mother discouraged me from developing relations with girls, except in my own head that's not the complete or good explanation. I did date a lot of girls when I was a teenager. I was very active on a social level—school dances—and I would say I was rather popular around the girls in high school. I left high school, went into the service and in college, then that faded out—probably you were required to be more active with girls as you entered your 20s, and maybe I started to withdraw then—once again, I really wasn't that interested. I don't really know why I'm gay. I don't know why I would have been straight—had I been straight. I understand why I have a cool or negative outlook on sex in general—I understand that better—my family discouraged sex, having a very puritan attitude toward that. Not growing up with people who had an open attitude toward sex organs, toward boys and girls, and so on—I understand that. The gay aspect *per se* I don't quite understand. I did have a narcissistic element as a child—supposedly that's part of this picture. What it means I don't know.

Being gay, I'd say, has had a lot of advantages for me, and I'm not at all bitter about it. For that reason I think it helped me overcome my social insecurity, helped me feel liked. It has made possible for me to meet a lot of interesting people that I would not have met had I been a straight married guy with a wife and kids. So I've had a lot of advantages from being gay. I think I know a lot of people who I appreciate, people I share interests with. I know how to meet people socially—being gay means you have access to a lot of people I would not have had access to. So those have been advantages.

Possibly I've missed out a little bit in terms of everyday or superficial comfort, or caring for, or a wife cooking meals for me, but those are minor things. And possibly I've had a little bit—not anxiety—but a little bit of tension professionally, especially my first couple of jobs—worrying about what's my image going to be at the office, especially working in business—are they gonna suspect I'm gay? I used to worry about it a little bit. Would there be pressure on me to put on a heavy straight role at office parties, departmental affairs? I don't worry about that any more. My teaching situation does not create much pressure of this kind. So the disadvantages have mostly disappeared the way I see it now.

I suspect that what I told you so far gave you a blander picture of me than may be warranted. I probably perform socially rather nicely. I seem almost like an average guy within the context of my work, social station, and so on. Maybe there are some characteristics that would stand out if people get to know me, or—let me put it this way—all my close friends would say that I'm much more individualistic than most people, straight or gay. So people who know me would say I am hung up on independence, personal self-sufficiency, almost to the point of being paranoid. They would say that I'm extremely keen on preserving my individual freedom to do this and that. I'm more than average rebellious against authority, against social pressure toward conformity—and maybe partly because I need to preserve those aspects of my lifestyle that are unconventional, including being gay. Beyond that it probably has developed into a philosophical, political attitude on my part.

I'm into individualistic philosophies. I would ascribe to a sort of *laissez-faire* philosophy, which is the technical term for individualistic type of behavior. It is also a reflection of my general attitude toward people, toward myself. Very keen on individual freedom and very much opposed to all kinds of governmental and social pressures toward conformity—things that reduce our individual freedom. In social situations some things like that come up. If I'm in a group situation I get a little bit uptight about pressure toward conformity, and some would say I'm starting to worry about conspiracies. Well, it's a half joke but I have a little bit of that instinct. If I go out with a group of people I get a little worried that they will take charge and I'm not going to be allowed to speak up—outvoted—and I'm going to be pushed into doing things that I don't want to do, and certain things I'm very fussy about; and I would sort of raise the issue.

I refuse to cooperate on some trivial thing. For example, they all say we have to sing happy birthday—it's someone's birthday—I say I'm not gonna to sing, that's a collectivist type of idea. I'm not gonna be part of this group thing, I'm not a sing-along person, I'm not a go-along person, and I refuse. And they'll say, "Oh, come on. It's a trivial matter."

At school I would rebel if they started pushing us, for instance to give to charities that come around the school. Once it even happened they appointed me to be in charge of the United Fund Drive. It was really a dilemma for me. The Dean assigned me to take charge of the United Fund procedure in my department. I finally decided I'm gonna tell him that I don't want to do it or find an excuse for not doing it. And I had philosophical reservations about this. I don't want to be supporting any particular movement, charity, politics or any classroom situation to promote some political ideas. That's an unfair misuse of authority, and if I were a student I would be very furious. I would start a campaign against that teacher who tried to push me into a certain conviction. And that shows up sometimes socially and I would rebel in trivial social matters. Probably reflects what I would call a slightly bitter extreme, now and then.

Sometimes I would show sudden anger, which people are not prepared for. Most people think of me as being almost on the bland side—smooth, easy going, slightly reserved, a guy who does his own thing, who is basically agreeable. Then I would be these flashes of a different personality. Some people get puzzled by it. What does it mean? We don't know this side. I do have aggressive instincts. I think generally I control them. Once in a while they flare up, and I rarely have any real disasters. I might offend a few people now and then by taking too sharp a stand on a social-political issue, or something involving family tradition—a very cynical statement about church or religion—if I don't know the people they could be very irritated and possibly hold a grudge. By and large I get away with it.

I pursue a certain cynicism all the way through—maybe I should add that. Most people who know me would say that he's into a very cynical bag, that he takes pride in being cynical, pride in putting down conventions. He overdoes it possibly. He likes the cynical image because he wants to seem tougher than he really is. Underneath he's fairly idealistic and romantic and kindhearted, except he has gotten hung up on this thing. He wants to be nasty.

Chapter 11

Frank
Father of four and closeted

Frank is a 49 year old banker born in 1928 and living in the Midwest. He was married for nine years and has four children. Faced with a few close suicides and negative reactions from his brother, Frank tries to manage the complexity of his life by remaining closeted to his family and colleagues. Until his children came to live with him, Frank and his lover lived in a monogamous relationship, but then went their separate sexual ways. While they lead independent lives now, they still view themselves as part of a close relationship and an occasional sexual one.

FAMILY MEMORIES

My father was a very nice man with whom I enjoyed a very good relationship in the later years in my life. I don't feel that the relationship in the early years was very good. My brother was seven years older than I was and he was a very successful golfer. My father was a member of the golf club, and I would call my family upper middle-class, not wealthy by any means, and my father took great pride in my brother's achievements. I think that as a young person, perhaps at the age of 9, 10 or 11, I was seeking to find my place, my niche where I could excel. Unfortunately for me, my brother at that point was 16, 17, or 18, and had achieved a degree of success in athletics. There was a great deal of pride on my father's part—and rightfully so. I was trying to work at tennis and probably needed some help and guidance and lessons, and my father did not encourage me and would not offer me the assistance that a child of 9, 10 or 11 needs. I really needed lessons. I needed a club to be a member of.

Later, I went to work for my father and, in essence, proved that I could excel in certain areas which were, at that point in time, in production, in doing business. I was a very major producer for his firm, for this small firm, and I guess he began to realize, or recognize, that perhaps in one way or another, I also was able to achieve and do things—I am a motivated person, I do wish to achieve and try to achieve.

My mother and father were not terribly happy. They never got divorced because I don't think one did it in that day and age. I think, in essence, he regarded me as mother's favorite, therefore, not his. And I think the affection that he felt he gave to my brother. I think he felt my mother was sort of taking care of the affection for me.

I think probably the one way that I am most like him is in that he was a motivated person, he had drive. And I also am motivated and have drive. I am most certainly not like him in my conservatism. Perhaps to a degree in personality. He was a very personable man. People liked him and he made a very good impression publicly, and I think I do too.

My mother was protective of me, perhaps too sympathetic. I think in many instances I should have been getting a kick in the rear end instead of getting sympathy. She was always sympathetic, and "don't worry about it", you know, "this will turn out alright," etc. instead of saying, perhaps, "well, maybe you'd better do something about it, you'd better find a solution."

She's a very gentle person, very self-centered—self-centered, but not demanding. Let's put it another way. I think that her way of getting attention for herself was not a demanding way, but simply a way that requires sympathy and understanding. Not terribly intelligent probably, but certainly well read, well versed, went to plays, understands.

My relationship with her was and continues to be very good. I have no—please understand when I say that perhaps she should have been more demanding of me, that's something looking back from here. I have the greatest of fondness of her. I realize that she was, perhaps, trying to compensate for what I think she felt was my father's lack of attention, and she certainly has been a very satisfactory mother. I do not believe that she really tried to turn me against my father, but I think she wanted me to be on her side, so to speak.

In later years, when my mother and father did have problems, my brother and I discussed it very frankly and honestly. We would both come to a conclusion and we would talk to our parents—I, usually to my mother; he, usually to dad—and say "Look, the two of you have to settle this. This is the way it has to be done." We would try to, at that point, impose what we considered our wisdom on them.

The way that I am like my mother, in terms of personality, is that I am not a very demanding person, unless I have a very specific attitude or desire or need. If there is something that I want—that I particularly want—I am not only demanding, I will be almost unreasonable, if I think

I'm right. But for the most part, in day-to-day things, I will avoid confrontation, and that is much more like my mother than my father. My father enjoyed confrontations; I avoid them, I try to conciliate, to find a middle ground in my relationships with people, and in essence, I'm just not demanding.

I had almost no relationship with my older brother during the early years of our lives. He went into the Navy in 1942 at the age of 21 and I was 14. He was away at college, of course, from the age of 18 until 21, and that would make me 10 to 14. There was no relationship whatsoever, I mean, I was the little kid brother with nothing in common.

When I was about 18 my brother was 25, he had been married and his first wife died of asthma. She was perhaps three or four months pregnant. He was very shaken up by that, it was his childhood sweetheart. He came back on leave from the Navy where they had been together. And I guess during that two weeks that he was on leave he visited me at college and we went out several times—perhaps spent the first real time together, on a more or less man-to-man basis. We got along very, very well and I think from that time on we had a relationship which continues to be extraordinarily friendly and with very few problems.

About fifteen months after his first wife died, he did get remarried, to his first wife's best friend, to a young lady who he had known for the same length of years, I mean, all his life. Except that she had always been the other girl. He has been married to her for almost thirty-two years. It's a very happy, fine marriage.

EARLY SOCIAL AND SEXUAL MEMORIES

I think the first recognition of sexuality was probably in those sessions at Boy Scout camp when I was around 13. But I was late in dating, perhaps that is something, that's something in my proclivities at that point in time. I took out girls that were very socially acceptable. Mostly in the same social group as my parents. But I did start dating when I went to college in 1946. Continued to date a couple of girls that were from the social group, necked, but did not have sex, intercourse, until I think, I was something like about 20.

One of my friend's father decided he was going to fix up his son and myself, who were obviously backward, right—so he took us to Sally Stanfords in San Francisco. Sally Stanfords was one of the most famous madams in San Francisco. And this old character who was—he really was a character—he was divorced from the other boy's mother, and he picked up three girls and took them back to his apartment; that was it. He put the girls to work on the two of us, and so on and so forth—my first sexual experience. And looking back at it I look at it as being funny. I may have been frightened—I probably was—but it worked. It wasn't of great interest to me. I didn't really therefore say, "Oh, my goodness, something has dawned on my life that is magnificent," so I didn't really pursue women. I went over to Korea and I did then when the occasion presented itself. You would go on R&R and you would go with other officers. They would be going to whorehouses, and you went with them, etc.

Then I came back from Korea and I got married. I was married when I was 22 or 23, in 1953. No, I'm wrong. I was almost 26. We were married for nine years. It was a very difficult marriage. It went, as most do, fine at first. I married a very wealthy girl, very spoiled, very demanding, and at the same time, unfortunately, mentally ill. Her mental illness has become obvious later and she, in fact, went to a clinic and has been there for some six years, which is why my children have been living with me for those six years. But at that point in time I did not recognize it and no one did. The illness was one of being afraid to be out in society. From the beginning, the evidence of withdrawal from society was not something that was terribly apparent, but as the years went by we would have to refuse more and more social obligations, until finally we would almost not go out to any social obligations, except to the very best of friends' houses. No large parties—nothing that involved. She simply could not cope with larger numbers of people. It was a part of withdrawing from society.

That particular problem did cause friction between us because I was in a business which required social contact and which for my success was necessary. It became a problem for us. She became more and more demanding of my time. She did not wish me to spend time at my golf course, my hunting club, away from the house, etc. In other words, she wanted me with her as much as possible, but was unwilling to do these things with me that I wanted to do. Those, in essence, were the largest problems that we ran into.

We lived across from a park which was somewhat notorious, but it hadn't bothered me. We had lived there for three years, and I guess in that last year before my divorce I walked the dog and someone would stop me. Instead of saying no I would say OK, and I had a homosexual experience and rather liked it. Sex was difficult at home—not satisfying, and I'm sure that was my fault. It was an adventure in a dark park. There was a sense of guilt and I think I did not do it again for three months. But, at the end of three months, again, I decided to try, and it became something that I did more and more often. This would have been around 1960.

I did feel guilty, afterwards. But after a year, I guess, from perhaps the first experience and then abstaining for three months and then slowly but surely doing it more often, I came to look at myself. I think perhaps the one thing I can be is very honest with myself, and I said, I'm not really happy at home. I also recognized that although I had not had homosexual contact with a man previously, that there had been an inclination previously, because I had admired the male body and had bought magazines and so on. I didn't buy pretty girlie magazines, I bought boy magazines. And I simply said why should I—realizing that there would be a problem from the standpoint of my social life—why should I be unhappy in my sexual life. And that is really what determined me to get the divorce.

After I divorced her, we had a bitter disagreement for about the first year, after that we became quite good friends. She remarried after approximately two years. The man that she married was willing to live on her money and they, in essence, withdrew to a tiny little village in the Northeast. She was able to withdraw, which was what she was seeking. Unfortunately, that gentleman must have been unbalanced because he began to play sexually with my older daughter. She did not say anything. However, after about a year she asked if she could go away to high school, and she did go to a private coeducational school. She came home on a Christmas break and her sister, my youngest daughter, told her that the husband was making advances sexually toward her. At that point the older one felt she had to say something to her mother. She told her older brother, and the older brother and she went and told their mother what was happening, and she phoned me. That was the beginning of a very unsettling experience. The gentleman committed suicide when confronted with this information. My ex-wife completely withdrew and broke down, and could not be treated here and went to the clinic.

When I became divorced I really didn't know homosexual people or the life. I really knew nothing. So I went to bars, but I wasn't terribly comfortable in bars at first. Having been married for some nine years, I had become used to the home life and the sociable home life. So I was seeking a more, more of a—somehow or other, I knew it had to exist—a home life in the homosexual milieu. But I finally met a few people who began to show some aspects of a home life and of how people lived in a homosexual milieu.

The one experience I remember is going into a gay bar and having two of my best friends honking and waving at me from a car. Heterosexual friends, mind you, a married couple. Fortunately, they did not know it was a gay bar, but all of a sudden you're starting to say, what's going on here, this is a small city, I know a lot of people. A little bit later—and putting it into perspective twenty years later—I went to the theater with two fellows, and two rows in front of me were my aunt and uncle and in the row in back of me were a cousin and his wife, sitting there. And I was with two guys that were gay, and that made me uncomfortable. Other things like that happened, so I was delighted to move away.

So, I moved to a much larger city. I was careful to be seen then, initially, at enough social events and dinners, large dances, with ladies, where I knew I would be running into people I would know. This would establish my reputation as being somebody who went out and saw girls, and so on and so forth, but my own homosexual life at first centered around the bars. I didn't know any people, but it didn't take me long to begin to know people and meet them and establish a social life.

About 1963, I had, in fact, met someone and been living with him. We were together for four years. My ex-wife came down to visit me one time. She was introduced to him and I believe that he said something. He did tell me later that he had said something, but unfortunately he was not always to be believed. He said that he told her that he was a homosexual, that I was a homosexual, that we were lovers, and that she didn't have any chance of getting me back, which, I think, had entered her mind at that particular point. I have never said anything to my ex-wife about my homosexuality. Nor has she ever said anything to me. I presume that she told my brother, because I do not know how else he could have learned. I've been relatively circumspect.

My brother visited from San Diego on a Saturday, having called me in advance, and said, "I'd like to see you, but away from your home," and we met at a hotel and he asked me if I was a homosexual, and I probably made the mistake of saying yes, because I think if I had to do it over again, I would have said no. And I said, "Yes, I am", and he said, "Well, I think it can be an extreme detriment to your career, and I think it is very bad for your family," meaning the children. And he said, "I wish that you would consider seeing a psychiatrist." Well, I realized that I had made a mistake, from the standpoint of my life, from the standpoint of believing that my brother would accept it. I had, in fact, misjudged. So I said, "Fine, I'll see a psychiatrist," and I did, once. I went to a friend, and he said, "Are you happy?" and I said, "I'm very happy" and he said, "But you don't want your brother to consider or believe that you're homosexual," and I said, "Yes, that basically is true," and he said, "Well, then I have only a few suggestions. What would be the things that your brother would consider as completely nonhomosexual?" And I said, "Well, like golf, athletics, sports," and he said, "Fine, do you enjoy playing ...?" and I said, "Yes, I enjoy playing golf," and he said, "Well, join a country club, go to football games, tell your brother that you went to a psychiatrist, and let him draw his own conclusions." That's what I did, that's what I do—although I do enjoy the athletics, football games—and it's fine. He has never asked me since. And there we are.

CURRENT SITUATION AND EXPERIENCES

I had been with my first lover from 1963 until 1967. I told him I was unhappy in the relationship and I was finished. I bought back the house from him that I had bought for us both in the first place—I bought back half of it, and sent him off to an apartment. He wanted to get back together, but I had in the interim met Mike. Many of the things that I saw in Ralph, my first lover, that I did not like, I saw in Mike as complete opposites. He was a successful person, a well-educated person, a bright person, motivated and responsible. Motivated and responsible I think are two words that would not apply to Ralph, and I told Ralph that I had met someone that I liked and that we were going to get together, and—he committed suicide, Ralph. It was unfortunate.

I had done the very best I could to be gentle and be careful not to hurt him, realizing that I was the one who was unhappy and had to tell him, and I had told him many times that I was unhappy. He continued to do the things I did not like, which were in essence, go out away from me with many, many other people. I did not accept that at that time and I did not approve and did not want it to happen.

In any event, Mike and I did get together. We lived together for approximately four years before my children came to live with me in 1971. At all times, because of his occupation and mine—and he is ten years younger than I, by the way—we maintained separate households although we lived together. We would either be in one or the other. We maintained separate addresses—he has an apartment at the shore and I had a home in the city. When the children arrived we talked about it, we knew they were coming. We had just bought a brand new home, that was the perfect house that we wanted to live in. We loved it, but he never moved in. The children and I moved in. We discussed it—we decided that we would adjust our lives as best we could to the fact that I had the responsibility of the children. So during this period of time, the children lived at home and I stayed at home, period, with them and a housekeeper. I saw Mike on weekends, had dinners every Friday night, every Saturday night and every Sunday. I would stay overnight at the shore maybe one night out of every two months. We would take three or so weeks vacation during the summer and usually one week in the winter together, and we have continued to do that during the entire seven years that my children have lived with me.

Now the youngest is off to college, we are starting again to go back to the way we used to, which is living part of the time together in the city and part of the time together at the shore, although we by no means stay with each other every night of the week. We usually are together two or three nights a week. We both, I think, enjoy our independence. We certainly didn't do this before the children arrived, but I guess we've learned to live apart and we have a very good relationship—really, an extraordinarily good relationship. We talk to each other at least once a day, sometimes twice. As I said, see each other every Friday night, every Saturday and all day Sunday and maybe a Tuesday and Wednesday night.

I think probably we'll stay much the same as we are. My daughter, the youngest, only started college in September, and we're just beginning to adjust to this new thing, and then of course, you know, it's not going to be terribly permanent because they arrive home after Thanksgiving, for a month and a half, then go away again for four months and they're back again for the summer.

They know him. He is Uncle Mike to the kids. He was before they came to live with me. They met him and knew him then. We have made real estate investments together which have been very successful. He is looked upon as my best friend and as my partner in real estate investments. It is a substantial investment, and I am very careful to discuss investments with my children, and since it involves a substantial amount of money, they understand why there would be a close relationship between the person who is your partner in such large business ventures.

This has not been a source of difficulty for him. He is an extraordinary person and was willing to put up with it over the period of time. We had a very good relationship when the kids arrived. In addition to having a very fine relationship, we're two intelligent people who have a desire to keep it together, and as a consequence we make adjustments—each of us.

If we go to the theater we always have four tickets and we most usually go with gay ladies. But, otherwise we would go out with other gay men, or with other gay men and gay ladies—we have a lot of lesbian friends. Where it was necessary for business for him or for myself, socially, to be out with girls, we would do so.

The relationship on both our parts was completely monogamous until my children arrived. It was a very specific part of the discussion prior to their arrival—we had one week's notice. We talked about it because he knew how I felt, he knew the reason I had left Ralph. One of the things I said to Mike was that I understand fully that my children are going to be living with me for the next several years. We have decided that we're going to live apart and not impose what is our homosexual life on those children, and I said I understand completely that you have to have a sex life away from me, so I ask only one thing—do it—don't talk about it, don't tell me about it, and let's not bring it up in front of our friends. And that, basically, lasted until the last couple of years when our attitudes began to change, in that we became more realistic of what was going on, on both our parts, because I didn't have very many opportunities to do anything away, so I didn't very often.

But on the other hand, when the opportunity arose, I took advantage of it sexually; I knew he was, and we talked about it. We were very open about it among ourselves, so we simply said if this is our lifestyle, let's recognize that it is and as a consequence we have learned now to go on some occasions to bars together, to go to separate sides of the bar and pick up people and take them our own separate ways, and so on and so forth.

His affairs have not made me feel uneasy, nor do I think there have been any that I have had that have made him feel uneasy. I can give you an example of what I consider to be the openness of our discussing. We were in Germany together, and Germany is marvelous sexually. We went to the bars, we were living in a hotel room together. But one or the other of us would go home with someone we had picked up and the other one would take somebody to our hotel. One of the fellows that Mike met over there came here and stayed with him down at the beach, and that was fine. It didn't bother me. But Mike brought him to a dinner at a friend's house. There were only seven of us and this young German was being very affectionate towards Mike. That was fine, the evening ended—two days later we had our chance to talk. I said, "I am not jealous, I'm not upset or anything, I just think it's wrong to do that in front of our friends." He said, "I understood and I agree with you, and it won't happen again."

We still have sex, but rare, rare. You know, I feel like the little fellow, you know, in the schoolroom, or in a big class in college, and the man says "How many people have sex once a year?", and he waves his hands and says, "Me, me", and the professor says, "What are you so happy about?", and the guy says, "Well, tonight's the night" (laughter). The reason that I'm laughing is that Mike and I had sex last weekend. But it is rare—it's probably once every couple of months.

If we are together, we sleep together, and we hold each other—we snuggle and hold each other—but the outward exhibitions of affection, in public, I mean even at parties or dinner parties, we no longer hold hands. We kiss each other in the morning or at night.

Chapter 12

George and Harold
Twenty-five years and monogamous

George and Harold are the only couple interviewed. George, born of Jewish immigrant parents in 1927, is a 52 year old attorney and Harold is a 45 year old vice-president of a marketing research firm who was born in 1934. They have been together for almost twenty-five years since 1954 and have a monogamous, compatible, and happy relationship. George talks about his introduction to homosexuality as a 14 year old delivery boy, but it wasn't until college that he, like Harold, fully understood what it all meant. It is Harold who discusses their relationship in more depth and who points out George's unhappiness in not fully achieving his life's goals.

GEORGE'S FAMILY MEMORIES

My father was a salesman in the dry goods business. We had limited funds, but funds that we did have we used for the education of my sister and myself more than anything else, so we were given musical training and religious training, and things like that. We always went to museums with both of my parents. My father had a limited education, but when I say that, he went to work at any early age so he did read a great deal. Not literature so much as the newspaper, the Yiddish newspaper.

He was the breadwinner more than a father. My mother really ran the household and the family more than he did, although he was influential in running the household. My mother was the stronger one, not only in our family, but she had several sisters and brothers, and in her family she was probably the strongest one of all the sisters, she was the one that all of the other sisters came to with their troubles. In that sense she was not domineering, but dominating—domineering in that sense—and whatever she generally wanted to do everyone went along with.

My parents have never kissed one another in front of anyone. When he came home in the evening my father never kissed my mother. The only time they ever greeted one another that way was on a holiday and the whole family would do that. Even now, there's only my sister and I alive, and we don't greet each other with kisses, so we're not a kissing family. He was always concerned and we knew of the love for one another, but he didn't know how to really react to children.

Both my sister and I were pretty good kids, and there was a minimum amount of disciplining for us. We did take private music lessons and other things, and I think the only thing was forcing us to practice, and that was more or less my mother's thing. My mother might discipline us or she might wait for my father, but we were very rarely disciplined, very rarely.

On the surface it seemed to me to be a good marriage. The only fights were about money, and that's because of the Depression. The only arguments were about money because my father would help out people from time to time. We didn't have that much money that my mother felt he ought to be helping out other people, but he always said they were in worse straits than we were. But other than that, there was never any argument about going someplace or this wasn't done or that wasn't done.

My father was not very talkative about his feelings or his attitudes, and he didn't talk too much unless he had a real opinion. I don't think I talk too much either, unless I'm opinionated. I don't know whether I'm like him. He was always late—but I don't think I'm late like he—he was proverbially late. He was late for his own wedding; got a flat tire on the Brooklyn Bridge. But he was always last minute getting dressed. To a little bit I'm like that, but I think in the last ten years I've improved tremendously so I'm not that way.

My mother was a very good housekeeper, very good cook. She also helped my father financially, at a time in the middle of the Depression when things were really rough. She had been a seamstress as a young girl, before she even married my father. My father through friends was able to get her piecework outside. He got her a sewing machine so she did piecework in the house, which supplemented the family income, and in the evening my father and I would help her. My sister was not one to help on that, although we could pull her in on it. My mother was very good at that. She was also, as I said before, the one that all of her sisters always went to when there was a problem.

She was also an immigrant like my father. But she had, being a girl, less education than my father and also her father had lots of girls in the family. My grandfather was not a real breadwinner. His daughters supported him more than he supported them. He was a scholar in that sense, both my grandfathers were Talmudic scholars. They were not rabbis. So I think that training passed on to me through my parents. Both my parents had great respect for education.

GEORGE'S EARLY SOCIAL EXPERIENCES

I was a very good, well-adjusted kid, and a very nice kid. And I never caused any trouble for my parents or for my relatives. We have a close-knit family on my maternal side and I have cousins my own age so we're very close to one another. Of course we've gotten more separated because they've gotten their own families and such. But we still are very close to one another and get along very well with everybody.

I had a natural instinct for sports. I'm not the best sports player but I have a natural ability. Some kids are awkward at it and I was never awkward in sports. I liked sports. In fact, as a child I used to sneak into the ballpark underneath the gate. I used to walk the ballplayers—in those days ballplayers had to take the subway, they didn't have any money and I would walk with them from the ballpark to the subway because they were my big heroes.

I also had musical studies and I had religious studies. I just didn't have time to have a close friend. I got home from school at three o'clock, then I had to go to religious school in the evening and then I would come home and have supper. I had to do my homework, and then I had to practice the violin or else I had to practice violin at seven o'clock in the morning. And the other kids had leisure time because they might not go to religious school or they might not practice the musical instrument.

I went to a very exciting high school, a school with boys who were intellectually very superior. It was not coeducational. It really took a lot of work just to keep up with them. I was not at the top of the class. You had to take an examination to get into that school, and I was admitted and I went there and the second day I was there I was very frustrated. Completely frustrated because these kids in the class just rattled everything off and I came home totally frustrated by it and said to myself, "What the hell am I doing in this school with all these geniuses? I'm not one of them." And I cried in my pillow and somehow during that night I said to myself, "Well, what the hell, they let you in. As long as they let you in, you're in. Let them throw you out. And you just fight your way through and do the best you can. You won't be at the top of the class, but you do damn well. You'll do as well as you can, if they want to they'll throw you out." And I lasted.

I made the decision to stay myself. Because I wanted to—as long as they let me in, then I knew I had passed the basic requirement and if they wanted to they could throw me out. But I wasn't going to resign.

GEORGE'S EARLY SEXUAL MEMORIES

Sexuality I found about in street talk. Even masturbation I didn't know anything about that at all. I guess as I approached puberty, which was late, I was rather hairless and as a child I would in fact use an eyebrow pencil, something like that, to paint on hair. But I did not masturbate or anything else. Because I just had never done it. Although I must have had wet dreams. I may have tried to masturbate but I didn't know how to do it. So I never climaxed except possibly with wet dreams.

When I was say 13 or 14, I had gotten a job as a delivery boy for a grocery and I was delivering orders and getting, I don't know, 15 or 25 cent tips for boxes of groceries—this was around 1940 or so. One time I made a delivery and the doorman suddenly kissed me and I said, "What the hell's wrong with you?" or something like that. And he said, "Oh nothing, you just remind me of a friend." And so I let it go at that. And then I made further deliveries there and he offered me money for a sexual act. I don't know what it was exactly. Anyway, one time I got desperate. I'd never had any sexual act and I think what happened is he paid me to put my hand on his penis. And that was fine. And then he asked me to go to his place and offered me something like $5 or $10, which was a good size money in those days, which after due deliberation I decided to accept. I went to his house and, I don't know whether he jerked me off or what happened, or whether he just jerked off with me there. I found this a very lucrative way of getting side money and I started calling upon him regularly, at least once a week, and got paid for it. I think the most that would happen, well, we did undress. And I probably masturbated him and I think that he masturbated me. So that's my first sexual experience. And that went on for quite some time. In fact, at one point I used to get so much money from him, and he was a poor doorman as it was, that he said, "Don't come around so often." So, anyway, that was that. And then we—I think we, I decided, this is silly, I don't want any part of it. And I stopped it.

At some point or other I went into the Navy and I guess at that point I started masturbating by myself because I found out about it and enjoyed it. So I masturbated—I never did it with any other boys. There was never any mutual masturbation or anything like that.

There wasn't too much social life with girls. We didn't have many parties except birthday parties, things like that. There weren't too many, you know, when you're 14, 15, 16, at that age there just weren't, in that period of time, which is the early 1940s. I don't think the social life was what it is today. I think it was quite different. And I think boys stayed together and girls stayed together. Maybe I'm wrong.

I did go in the Navy and there's a lot of sexual talk in the Navy. I did have two experiences with a WAVE who I met and had some sexual experiences with her which were satisfactory. And as far as homosexual activities went, I had one homosexual experience at the Naval Hospital. That was with an x-ray technician on an x-ray machine. It wasn't very successful. In fact, at a certain point somebody knocked on the door, so it was very disruptive and I didn't like it at all.

The only sort of sexual activity I had in the Navy with anyone else was one very young, attractive fellow, about the same age as I was. We were both rarely on base together so we never had any time for contact, and one night we were on base together. He was in his bunk and I started going over to his bunk and talking to him and started almost to play with him. And at that point I—my friends called out that they're going into town, "Come on, let's go into town," and that was the end of that thing. That night we went into the local bar and there were always girls around who we always fooled around with. I fooled around with two whores, but I never went to bed with any of the whores although I did feel them up. They were really, really gross.

Now, as far as coming out, I went to college in 1946 when I was 19 and was taking an English course where I met somebody who was attracted to me and whose advances I was not willing to accept. It was not a physical advance, it was a social advance, saying, "Come over and have a drink." And I did come over and he introduced me to his house. He invited me to dinner. He, at that point was living, still is living with another fellow, they've been going together now for more than thirty years. And they had an open situation at that time and they did invite a lot of people around. And at one point he invited another boy whom I found attractive. One of the basic reasons why I went with him is religious, because he also was Jewish and I think that made me accept the fact. And I did go to bed with him and performed homosexual acts which I found acceptable. I mean I'd engaged as a passive homosexual, in passive homosexual acts with the doorman, so I knew what they were all about. And this is the first time I responded positively to them.

I didn't fight these impulses too hard. The person who introduced me was older. At that point he was in his late 20s. He'd been a lieutenant commander in the Navy. His own education had been interrupted because of wartime. He was one of the first ones inducted into services, so he was old only in the sense of being a returning veteran. But he really wasn't old. He was old in comparison to 18 and 19. I was disturbed by my willingness to go forward with it, until I discovered their world.

We used to go over to these two girls' house, two girls living together. And they used to have a Sunday dinner, and at the Sunday dinner a group of intellectuals gathered. And some of these intellectuals, you might call it a salon of a sort, but the people who were there are now the leading poets in America. This was the early '50s, a fascinating time to be with them. And some of the people there have gone on to write hit plays, musical and straight plays, that have been very successful on and off Broadway. So it was intellectually stimulating to be there and fascinating to meet these people. And all of the people were, apparently all were veterans of World War II who had traveled a great deal and seen a great deal. Some of them had been to Paris and seen Gertrude Stein and some of them had been in the Pacific Coast all over the world, so they were interesting people, they weren't just kids out of high school. These are mature people who had returned to educate themselves.

Since I circulated with them, I did go to bars with them, including the famous Black Cat in San Francisco, where I often stayed until closing time every Saturday night. And from time to time I would find somebody interesting. I wouldn't just sleep around, it had to be somebody whom I imagined that I liked or accepted. And I would sleep with them. And then, at one of these Sunday salons, I met somebody. We became lovers, very serious lovers. But he got a Fulbright scholarship, so he had to go off on his Fulbright. I thought we were still lovers, but we drifted apart, so we went our separate ways. I had several other affairs but I didn't go for one night stands too often. And then I met my present lover and we've been together for twenty-four years.

GEORGE'S CURRENT SITUATION AND EXPERIENCES

My relationship with Harold is very positive. We enjoy each other's company tremendously and I think we make a very good couple. We have the same interests generally, although some of our interests vary. I'm more interested in sports and he is more interested I think in having the proper home, things like that. I like a proper home, but dressing up a bit doesn't matter to me so much as the comfort of it. We both like the theater; we both like good food. And we like each other and we like each other's company. We like the same people a great deal, although there are some variations on that.

We are very compatible sexually. Extremely compatible. So there's no reason to look for sex outside or even want it or even want it thrown at me to accept it. We have sex about three times a week or it might happen two or three times over the weekend, depending on the hour and how tired we are. We both work very hard.

We don't go to bars anymore because we feel that there's no reason for us to be in a bar. A bar is an alternative to living, to having a home. And we have a home, and if you go to a bar that would mean we're interested in somebody or something and we're not. And we're deadbeat to the bar unless we go with a group of friends, something like that. So we don't go out.

I've had some anxiety lately. My real anxiety, at night and what might create problems for me, or what keeps me awake anyway, or wakes me up early, is my concern for my ability to get work done and complete the work. I've got masses of work to do and I'm late on some things that should have been done, so it's a matter of being able to continue to service the clients properly and meet their needs, because they have needs and they have demands and that's the only thing a lawyer really has to offer—availability.

I'm not anxious about my age. I was absolutely delighted turning 50 because I thought it was an achievement to be 50. I'm somewhat young looking and I think I have a youthful outlook on life too, and I was absolutely delighted to be 50. In fact my lover threw a 50th birthday party for me, a surprise party for me. We had a room of about 80 people here who were truly not just people from anywhere, but they were friends and true friends—long standing—and it was one of the best parties anybody had ever attended.

HAROLD'S FAMILY MEMORIES

My father was a very vigorous man, physically very vigorous. Very strong man. Very strong willed. My father doesn't see grays; everything to my father is black or white. He was a street kid. He was, I think, out of his home when he was a child, 8 or 9—maybe living with relatives from time to time. So he's grown up on the streets. And he tends to see good and evil in a very biblical sense—not a religious sense—but biblical.

When I was first aware that he had an occupation, he was in the clothing business. He worked for a clothing manufacturer. He later went into his own business as a manufacturer, which failed. He then tended a bar. He was a union organizer, which was kind of interesting, because he made most of his money while he was in the clothing business, I'm convinced, doing favors for friends by keeping unions out of the business. He was quite successful financially, through the war years. I think a lot of it came from—I don't want to say gangster kind of work—but under-the-table efforts. Maybe even numbers-running.

I never really had a strong feeling for my father. My father was very tender to my twin sister and myself—he loved my sister very dearly. She was probably the son he'd rather have had—tomboyish kind of girl, very active, pretty child. I think it was always accepted I was my mother's son and she was my father's daughter.

I would say in the last ten years my relationship with my father is somewhat closer—much closer. For one thing, it's physically closer. My parents live two blocks away now. But I began to feel in the last ten years or so as they were getting older, that I probably didn't give my father a chance to know him better. He's a very interesting man, primarily because of what he lived through, what his life has been like. And I think his instincts have all been very good.

He idolized me. Because my sister no longer speaks to either one of my parents, he sees me as his only attachment to life. He does consider me fairly successful—he's proud of me. I can't say that I love him. I have a good deal of admiration for a lot of the things he's done. He's a man who I think very much likes to be liked by people and tends to go out of his way to make himself liked.

I don't think we ever really discussed sex. There was a point in my life, maybe around 1950, when I was about 16 when somebody, a friend of the family, suggested to my parents that I might be gay. He didn't believe it. My mother asked me in front of him. She said she wanted to talk to me and she asked me if I liked men. I wasn't sure that I did—I knew what she was talking about, but I really wasn't sure of my preference at that point, even though I had inclination. I wasn't really sure. And even if I had been sure I probably wouldn't have told them because I'm sure it would have hurt them. My mother is much more open to this kind of thing and recognizes that it exists, even more than my father, I think, even though there were known homosexuals living in our building when I grew up. My parents were very friendly with them. My father said, "See, I told you—it's impossible." I don't think we ever discussed sex other than that.

My mother, on the other hand, has tried to discuss my sexual life with me through the years, and for the most part I have tried to pretend that I didn't hear. Sometimes she has just needed to talk and she's needed somebody to listen. She has talked about her sex life. Apparently her life with my father is not very satisfactory.

Despite living for twenty-five years with some other man, I find it hard to believe that they don't know I'm gay. I'm sure my father doesn't. Somewhere it's here, in the back of my mother's head, and she refuses to bring it forth. Every once in a while I say to myself she must know, and then she'll ask me a question which just indicates to me that she doesn't— or certainly refuses to admit it.

I think I'm like my father—my father's a very pragmatic individual. In personality, my father is practical. He's quite a pragmatic individual; I like to think I'm that way. He is, I think, a realist, he's an extreme realist. I think in that way I'm like him. I also like to be liked by people. It's important for me to be liked. I also think that my father, unbeknownst to him, is a reasonably empathetic man, and he treats people the way he should be treated. He goes out of his way to be nice to people and not to offend them. I'm like him in that way, I would say.

My mother is very high strung, very emotional, nervous, and unfortunately those are the characteristics I've picked up from her. My mother is nine or ten years younger than my father. She felt, and I'm aware of this—I'm only aware of this because of the things she has told me about other men she has known or knew before my father—that she probably feels she could have done better.

She was sick quite a lot through her married life. The image I have of my mother and my sister (oddly enough I remember the same thing) is them lying in bed a lot. My mother was always getting sick and I think she was often getting sick when there was something to do that she didn't want to do. She also had shock treatment sometime in her early 50s, late 40s. I remember she went to a psychiatrist, sometime in her mid-40s, who wanted to give her shock treatment. I remember hearing a discussion and my father wouldn't allow it, and I guess I thought then, or thought later on, that it was something—a cure or help was being offered to my mother—that my father was denying; my mother had the same feeling. It was something I think he was afraid of, and many people would be.

I've only started to speak to my sister myself in the last six or seven years. She has not spoken to my parents for eighteen years. She apparently had great psychological difficulty in dealing with my mother and just after she was married apparently she had great difficulties with herself. I think at some point she said to herself I can deal with me and me alone, but I can't deal with me and mother. I think she had to be fairly sick in order to do this, but she did in fact divorce herself entirely from my mother and father. She has since discovered for herself that it was my father who was the problem and not my mother. She detests him. She adored him growing up. She says she detests him. And from everything she says now to me I think she does, and everything she sees in him she's quite correct. I think her reaction is violent. But she does not exaggerate what my father is like. It's part of everything being black or white—you must do this or can't do this, that kind of thing.

She talked to me about the possibility of sleeping with other women, but she is living with a man. She's a cruiser sometimes, I think, even at her age, in the same way that some male homosexuals are. I don't know if she is now, at least a few years ago she was. She seemed very sexually oriented, and she would think nothing of going to a singles bar and taking somebody home.

HAROLD'S EARLY SOCIAL EXPERIENCES

I was not sickly as a child. My health is generally good. I don't think I was particularly shy. I had friends, I made friends easily, but I never made a lot of friends. I always had a couple of good friends. Maybe I was sneaky, I don't know—I sometimes think about that, was I really all that good. I was very good at school, but I can't believe that—as I think back—that I wasn't a little sneaky. That imp quality that allowed me to get on very well with teachers. Teachers loved me. But I couldn't have been that good, and I'm sure I wasn't.

My sister and I, when we played games, we dressed up, both of us, as girls. We made dresses out of blankets or whatever was around, and the games were pretty much allied to movies that we saw. We did the Dolly Sisters one week. And there was a period of a couple of years, maybe a year, maybe two years, where we went through that. I don't think it was anything I brought into the street. I was aware at a certain point that my voice was possibly a little higher than the other guys, my walk may have been a little more feminine and then I corrected it.

I don't remember if somebody said something or what, but I do remember consciously correcting what may have appeared as being sissy. I don't think I was ever called a sissy, by anybody. My sister did. She would call me a sissy. My mother, now that I think about it, would often say, and it didn't have anything to do with being sissy, it had to do with being afraid of things, and I can remember her saying, "I should have named you Harriet," things like that. For example if she would be washing—giving us a bath and the water was too hot—I would get nervous and my sister wouldn't, she would say that. It had nothing to do with acting feminine, it had to do with being afraid of what I felt were perfectly natural fears, but I do remember her saying that.

I played streetball. Streetball was never a problem with me. I never played baseball. Maybe I played softball in junior high school, but not until I was at camp, and I was suddenly aware that I was rather inadequate there. The very first day, I remember at camp, we all went out to the softball field and I intentionally—I was 13—I intentionally wore regular shoes instead of sneakers so that I could get to the field and say I forgot my sneakers and go back to the bunk and not come back, which is exactly what I did. I never really learned to play ball that year, but I did discover that I was fast. I was great at track, all track events, so I was an important man on campus, but I was also in all the plays.

HAROLD'S EARLY SEXUAL MEMORIES

I will tell you one of the things I can remember, and I can remember it was almost like having a spark through me. My parents were lying in bed early Sunday morning and I was sitting next to my father on the bed and we were kind of playing. We were a very affectionate family group. And my father dropped my hand on what I thought was his erection. My hand fell there and I took it away, and I thought about it. And after that there were certain periods when my father was sleeping that I would try to grope him. I never said to myself at that time or I never thought that I liked men. I just wanted to have that feeling again.

I can remember waking up one night with an erection. It must have been in my early teens, lying in bed. My sister and I shared the same double room. I was on the top bunk bed and I can remember my mother coming into the room and saying to my father, "Come here I want to show you something." I wasn't really aware what she was going to say and suddenly I realized I had an erection. She was showing my father that I had an erection. So that, combined with the fact that I had touched my father's, and their obvious interest in mine—I think I sought my father out sexually. I wanted to have that feeling again. I wanted to feel that thing, that spark or whatever it was, and I remember being very conscious about having an erection at night and I would lie there in a way so that they could see it, again.

I think my first awareness of myself as a homosexual may have had to do with a couple of guys who lived in our building as we were growing up. This was around 1950 or '51. There were two guys who lived above us with one of the mothers, a sister, brother-in-law and children, and the two guys shared a room in this enormous apartment. And I used to babysit for the sister when they all went away. I must have been 15. Somehow we struck up a friendship with this guy. I was clearly attracted to him. I did not think of it necessarily as sexually, but I was attracted to him as an individual. He was not a feminine person at all. I used to think his friend was. Everybody in the building knew their story, including my parents, who did not discourage the friendship. They did not say, "You should not see this person, he is a homosexual." I became more and more aware of it as I got to know him better. He even tried to pass me along to a friend to meet me. He once asked me if I was gay or felt gay, or something like that. I said no, and I realized I did.

I didn't have a sexual experience until my second year in college. I started going to a gay bar, probably this was 1953 or so, with a friend who was not gay, he said, and there was somebody there who pursued me for a long time and I finally gave in.

I think I have had in my lifetime maybe fourteen or fifteen experiences. It's highly unusual, very freakish—like my job, having one job—having only one love. I don't know if I was counter-oriented sexually, afraid of it, or what. I enjoyed it when it came about and they tended to be for long periods.

I have not had any heterosexual intercourse. I dated girls, I've necked and petted, I've come close. I thought I desired it a couple of times, but I never actually had sexual intercourse, and you're the first person I've admitted that to. It's funny, even being gay I guess you want to be manly, you know, and somehow that's part of it.

HAROLD'S CURRENT SITUATION AND EXPERIENCES

I think when I first met my lover I was 19. I knew him for a year before we actually had any sexual activity. I used to see him in the bar from time to time and I used to go with a friend who was very promiscuous and I think I probably had my sexual life through him as much as anything else. And George used to be at the bar and talked to us, and finally we just got together. I met him at the beach one night and he asked me to go home with him. I said if you feed me first. He said sure, come on home, and from then on we saw each other.

We didn't move in together right away. George lived with his family, I lived with my family. I was still in school. I knew him casually for a year before we established a relationship. We saw each other on weekends. It kept up our interest, I guess. Also, when we finally did live together, he still had a very close relationship with his family—very close—and he would see his family a lot during the week. So even during the early part of our relationship when we lived together, we were not with each other constantly, and I think that also helped a good deal.

George is a dreamer. I don't think he is happy, in fact, I think he's truly unhappy, and as a result of that I think he takes a lot of his hostilities out on me, a lot of them. He's a kind of hostile individual, I think, in many ways. He had a very difficult time with his family life. I don't think he's achieved what he hoped to achieve in life. I think he's finally coming around to what he feels is a late stage in life, and maybe it is.

He was never poor, but he's never achieved, either financially, job wise, or culture wise. I think George would have loved to have a salon. He's part of that whole intellectual atmosphere. When he went to school it was very smart to be a poet, writers, dancers, and people in the arts, and I think he misses that in life. So I feel a tremendous restlessness in him. And as I say, it comes out in anger and hostility which he takes out on me.

He is terribly moody and often becomes silent, which I've often said is possibly the worst thing you can do to anybody, just not talk. I don't necessarily talk either, but I won't deliberately ignore or hide my feelings. I've always felt he was more attached to his family than to me. Now maybe that really isn't so. The evidence was there. He's used that as an excuse sometimes. Little things that I do trouble him and when I say little things, I mean really trivial things. Now obviously, those aren't the things that trouble him, but they trigger it.

I can remember my very first argument with George, at least my very first experience with him. He was not speaking to me for three days and I couldn't find out why and it turned out to be that I had left a dirty dish rag on the sink. George is hardly compulsively neat so it can't have been the dirty dish rag, but that's what triggered it and he reacted to that.

I'm not even sure how much alike we are. What we want more than anything else is to stay together and I know he cares for me a good deal, a great deal, possibly more than he's cared for anybody else in the world. I think that's been a problem too. I think I've never seen him affectionate with his family. I've never seen him kiss his sister. I don't remember him kissing his mother. I'm sure he's told you about his family and the difficult times that he's had with them, so sometimes I often think he resented me, not as an intrusion. Sometimes I think maybe I've kept him from moving on, in that he's wanted to stay with me and therefore didn't feel that he should do anything else.

We have never really separated. I have a temper. He thinks I'm overly glib—I'm only overly glib when I get angry and things have welled up in me. He says when we argue he can't argue with me because I come on too strongly and I say things too fast and too harshly, and he can't come back or combat it or either one. He's often said he's afraid of my mouth.

On the positive side—I'm trying to think of positive things. It's interesting, I can't really think of the positive side, except that we do often enough have wonderful times together. I love George's brightness. I'll tell you what I think troubles me with him, or used to trouble me about him—I think he's a little better than he was—he never let people know how smart he was. He kept to himself and still does to a degree—a kind of reserve, not as if he's observing. I wouldn't mind if he was observing, but what he's doing is ignoring. George can be very charming and he doesn't allow people to see it. I don't think people know him for the kind of person he is. Now that partially has to do with the fact that we share most of our friends, all of our friends. I try to encourage George to see people individually. He has never had—at least as long as he's lived with me—his own friends.

Our relationship is entirely monogamous. I'm sure it is on his part too. Our sex life is still fairly active. We enjoy each other physically. We do like doing it together. George likes doing things all the time, actually. When he's not doing things he's working. He can't sit and relax. Can't sit and read a book.

We have a house in the country, which I'm sure he's told you about. We used to take a house on Fire Island because George didn't want the country house. I forced him into the house, I realize. I know exactly how I forced him into it, because I appeared unhappy for long enough. It's lonely up there for him, and so he tends to work all day or else we go out driving. He's just not comfortable relaxing. It's an entirely relaxing atmosphere, but he doesn't feel relaxed. He's fine when people are over, when we're going out to see people, but he likes constant activity. Part of this may have to do with the fact that he feels that he has to live every moment. People get to the point where they say to themselves I want to enjoy what I have, just keep doing, I don't want to miss anything.

Chapter 13

Jim

Sissy, flappers, and a long-term roommate

Jim is a 55 year old former businessman, who now directs a large community agency. He was born in the East coast in 1923 and now lives in the West coast. He recalls his father's constant use of the word "sissy" for things he disapproved of. But it wasn't until Jim got out of the Navy in the 1940s that he began to explore gay bars and his own identity. For the past twenty-five years, he has shared his life with someone he calls a roommate. Against a background of "roaring twenties" parents, Jim's life emerges as one in which he consistently seeks control and tries to avoid disruptions.

FAMILY MEMORIES

My father was a man with great expectations and a lot of ability, but he didn't know how to fulfill them. He was the son of a very successful song and dance man on the stage. His father was a very well-known vaudeville entertainer. My father always seemed to be standing in a shadow, rightly or wrongly. He would always do his father's routines.

He was a tremendously capable salesman. He could sell an ice box to an Eskimo. He had a very outgoing, bubbly personality, but whether it was the times or himself, he managed to succeed and be well employed during the Depression when everybody else was broke. But he never achieved the kind of success during the time when he should have.

I developed a kind of disrespect for my father because I never thought he was strong. I resented him if he wanted to punish me. A typical example is when I was 5 and he took me to a bar. I was very tiny—I'm not the biggest person in the world now, but when I was young, I didn't think I'd ever grow. He would stand me on the bar and I could recite poetry at a time when I could barely talk. I was very good at it. I read precociously young. My older brother learned to talk at the time I was talking, according to my mother. For whatever reason, I was extremely interested in reading when very young, and I liked jingles and poetry, so it was a favorite occupation of my father's to stand me on a bar and show me off.

I'd always felt, in a sense, second best, because I was second born. I have an older brother—one year older—and they always dressed us like twins. They treated us like twins. Naturally, as the younger sibling, you got what was left over. Also, a great deal of fuss was made over my brother. He's taller, he was the swimming champion—all of these things. I withdrew from competing with him. Interestingly enough, it wasn't until the Navy required me to compete with him under a circumstance which is strictly a fluke, where they put us both in the same school, that I found I was extremely strong, reasonably bright, and was a damn good swimmer also. It was this experience in the Navy, where I had to be pitted against my brother scholastically on a par in the same classes, that I discovered that I had an ability to conceptualize in the abstract, particularly useful in mathematics, especially the higher types of mathematics. So there was an almost vicious delight, frankly, as an awakening where I'd help him with his homework. Until that time, everybody was telling everybody else how bright my brother was. Not that he isn't bright. But the relationship in my mind changed when we were put in competition and I won, when I did not expect to win.

My relationship with my mother was rather interesting. She's an extremely dominant woman with a very strong will, but we're a great deal alike. This whole business of not succumbing that I learned from my father, not to cry, I would also use it to my mother. But I'd know where it was coming from.

My older brother cried as a defense mechanism. When he was being particularly mean to me, I could dream up things for him to do that would get him into trouble, because I couldn't fight him. I tricked him into doing something. But I would never, never, yield to my mother.

It took a classic situation in my late teens when my mother was arguing with me about something, and I said, "I want to tell you something—I will not argue with you. I will never argue with you." Well, I would keep it at that basis, and what happened was that I could sense then she began to develop what I felt was a sense of respect. She leaned on me a great deal and confided in me in a lot of problem areas. I took charge of her financial affairs for her so that she would not have to worry about paying bills. She had an income that was regulated so that no matter how things were, everything was covered. Well, I was able to do this at the time. This took a burden off her. She had always been conscious of meeting her bills, and that was one thing that was bothering her. As a consequence, we developed a good rapport where I respected her for her total independence, in exchange for which I expected absolute total independence for myself and my life. There were areas that I told her I would not discuss, including homosexuality. I told her frankly I would not discuss it. Now, whether that's healthy or not, it wasn't a question of denying anything, I told her it was an area I would not discuss with her. We had a good relationship.

My mother never kissed. My mother was cold on the surface, and this is an interesting thing, because I was aware she was an extremely sensitive, emotional woman, but she seemed to lack the ability to emote. If you wanted to reach my mother you had to write to her. She was the kind of a woman who would be extremely moved to help people or children. She loved children. She absolutely adored having children around. She almost carried it to the point of a fetish in her later life. She had a collection of dolls. Some of them were actually life size, for which she liked to make their clothing. She would make clothing for other little children in the neighborhood. Very good at knitting and sewing but yet, she had this stone wall image that she presented to the public.

I also know that when my father would punish me, I would always make it a point never to cry when he punished me. My mother, in later years, said that this used to drive him up the wall and frighten him, because I would not cry as a child. In fact, I think about it in later years, because it almost made it impossible for me to express emotion. It was only many years later where I could even enjoy the luxury of crying. But I was aware of it, looking back at it, and I was aware of myself doing it at the time.

I can even remember saying to him once, "Don't you dare hit me". Now listen, we're talking about 5 and 6 years of age. And I don't know why I'd be that aggressive. I also remember, because we're talking about the 1929 period when some of this is going on, I became in my mind, a prude. My father had a lot of money during the Prohibition period, relatively speaking. We could afford to have someone in the house to clean, where you would have wild parties. They had all kinds of bathtub gin. My mother was a flapper and my father was the hottest thing in town as far as parties. They were the people you see in movies. They weren't the Gatsbys, but they paid for the parties and everybody came and did the Charleston. These parties in our home interfered with my sleep, interfered with my preconceived attitude toward parents. I resented it.

I was very fortunate that I had a fantastic grandmother. She was German, spoke very little English, and I spent a great deal of the early years with my grandmother because I was in the way while they were playing. Now, that's either a real fact, or it's one I certainly remember.

I admired my parents because I was aware that they were beautiful people. My mother was an extremely goodlooking woman and my father was extremely handsome, but I subsequently concluded that the only thing they did have in common is they were both goodlooking people. I'm sure that it was a kind of attraction which is meritorious, if you're heterosexual, to find each other physically attractive, But they had a lot of domestic strife. My father was extremely jealous—extremely jealous—and that was a constant typical pattern.

I would imagine my mother was a flirt to the extent that she was a stunning woman, a stunning woman. But I'm not sure that he had justification, because I'm also as keenly aware that my mother was extremely—very much—in love with my father. That is an observable fact that I have been aware of all my life.

But my parents separated. The main separation occurred while I was in the Navy, so I would say, 18. The thing that made it bearable was that my father was a traveling salesman. There were periods where he'd be away and, apparently in the lull, the returnings and the goings created, I assume, areas of harmony. They weren't constantly at each other. They would separate and come back, and then separate again. By this time my younger brother was born. He was eighteen years younger, and the struggle for survival became more poignant for my father. He was getting older, and was not the success that he wanted to be. He was also a great gambler. He'd lose a lot of money gambling, and this would create a hardship on my mother. When he had money he had lots of it, and when he had none he really had none. It would run very hot and very cold, with my mother attempting to maintain a standard of living during lean periods that would drive her up the wall and create tension. My mother was a very careful manager. She came from a rather poor German immigrant family, where her own mother scrubbed floors to make a living. My father was in a different category.

I think my relationship with my grandmother, my mother's mother, was particularly unique. I should not be remembering her as vividly as I do, and yet I remember everything about her, and she died about 1930, so I would have been about 7 or 8 years of age. I remember her home, her kitchen. I remember sitting on the garbage can under her sink. My eyes would follow her around. She spoke only German. I spoke German at that time. When she died they refused to let me go to the funeral, which they think was good for me, but I think was not. My father forbade me to speak German. In subsequent years I studied German and I have always kind of resented their interference with my relationship with my grandmother—real or imagined.

I got to touch a past generation very sensitively back in Germany through my grandmother, the songs she'd sing, the stories she would tell. She would always wear a long skirt. She was of another time. She would sit and grind her own coffee in her lap, or take you on the stoop to grind up horseradish. She had all the images of pleasant smells, of food, her own musty smell, which was apparently typical of older women of that Victorian period, who did not bathe that often. She had large, soft breasts; she must have been a midget, it seems to me. I know I wasn't the biggest kid and if she'd hug you, my head would be at her breast level. She must have been a very small woman. But I was keenly aware of her affection.

EARLY SEXUAL MEMORIES

I was very sexually aware from as far back as I can be aware. I was probably excessively precocious. I knew I could have an orgasm by the age of 8, but I was having sex for at least several years prior to that, with all the sensations of an orgasm, with little boys and little girls. There was no distinction in this early period. I was also keenly aware that sex was a pleasure. I was excessively uninhibited to the extent that I felt no guilt in my early carryings on. We're not talking about sex where you stick your penis in a maiden or something like this; it's merely sexual play.

I remember once, I must have been 7 or 8, having this little girl take her clothes off. She apparently went home and told her parents, and her parents came in and told my parents. I remember them coming into the house and they called me out into the kitchen. I remember me standing with my arms crossed on the cold linoleum floor, and my mother was sort of crying and carrying on: "He's only a little boy, he's only a little boy." My father then, after they all left, admonished me—strangely, ridiculously—and I can remember it: "Only sissies play with little girls."

Now the interesting thing about this comment was that I always remember, even at the time, that my father used the word "sissy" for everything that he disapproved of. He didn't want me to spend all my time reading at that time: "Sissies read." I asked to play the piano: "Sissies play the piano." I asked them if I could play the violin: "Sissies play the violin." I'm a good painter, but I began very early to make little drawings. My father objected to me doing this as being "sissy". The word "sissy" in my father's vocabulary was everything that was wrong, and constantly directed at me, at a time when I didn't know what the hell he was really inferring, except that it was always negative. The word itself then began in my mind to be associated with being effeminate, and we're talking about 8 or 9 years of age.

I was very aware in the neighborhood, at that time, of anybody who was a sissy was being called Mary Jane. Nobody called me Mary Jane. But that was the euphemism for someone being queer when you're 8 or 9 years of age. And yet, all the little boys played with each other. So it's very difficult to say in your own mind what it was that was characteristic of being a sissy. It was not sex at that time. It was being one who played with little girls or did all of the things my father disapproved of. But I knew that I liked all of the things my father said sissies do.

As a consequence, I developed an attitude about my father that he was wrong. Totally wrong. So either I was wrong or he was wrong, and it became a defensive thing to me. When he would forbid me to read around the house, I'd just go to the library after school and stay there. Then he'd see I wasn't out in the street getting beat up by the boys, or playing stick ball, and he would complain about that; he wanted me to fight. He always wanted me to be pugilistic and defend myself. I never got into that kind of situation. In fact he was telling me, since I was never going to be big, to kick them in the balls, before they get a chance. My temperament was not aggressive as a fighter. Now, I'm not a guy that runs away either, but I'm not somebody that goes out and smacks someone on the nose. It just isn't part of my temperament. I don't do this sort of thing. So I developed an attitude that my father was wrong.

The pressures of me being different were apparent because I wasn't doing anything really, I began to realize that I wasn't chasing girls, and even when I went into the Navy, I wouldn't drink, wouldn't go to a bar. I certainly wasn't going to go out with girls. I had a strange moral code which developed. I can look back at that now and say that moral code was kidding myself, because I wasn't having sex with men because I didn't know how—nobody asked me.

My fantasies were with people my own age. Men. It was more fun, because during the period of play, little boys didn't tell. Now, whether that was a factor I don't know. I can't evaluate that. In the early stages, I was experimenting with both. It didn't make any difference. But I felt more camaraderie with little boys.

There were experiences in the Navy which were betwixt and between, but these experiences were done as a defense mechanism. I would let people chase me until I caught them and then tell them not to do it again. Because, being very small when I went into the Navy, and very young, I just turned 17, I ended up with the nickname of the Cherry and everybody wanted to play grab ass. I was keenly aware that I was apparently a very attractive little kid. I was then able to use that. So I developed only a very aggressive method of sex while playing a very passive role in the sense of cruising. They'd think they were gonna get me, but I was always the one that finally got them, which is strange. It was done with a kind of coldness that was totally unsatisfactory because there was no emotional, romantic attachment to the affairs at all. It was like mutual masturbation, primarily to gratify me. I was aware of that, but I didn't know what else to do.

Then, when I was studying for my doctoral, I was about 28, life began to seem unreal. I was living in this total scholastic environment. I was sublimating. I was beginning to become aware of it. I was taking twenty or twenty-two units a semester. Even when I was going to school for the Navy, I was studying everything. I didn't have any time for relationships.

CURRENT SITUATION AND EXPERIENCES

I've been with my current roommate for twenty-five years, but he is not a lover in this classic cliche sense of the word. In fact, in recent years we don't even have sex. We have friendship. And I settled for something less than heaven by drawing up very basic guidelines. I must say I drew them up in my own mind and we discussed them. It takes years to work all the kinks out of them, but we developed a way of living with one another that required mutual respect and no embarrassment.

For example, we each have a veto on anybody who comes to the building. We don't drag "tricks" into the house. We even have a special facility, a special apartment downstairs that has doors to the outside. If you want to bring somebody home you bring them downstairs. If someone is introduced to the circle of friends that is someone you also might be having sex with and is introduced through the normal channels, that's acceptable. But not the idea of bringing tricks into the house, into the living area when no one's in the mood to see your tricks and see you carrying on. So by making the dwelling situation, the living situation, off limits for sexual activity, the ground rules worked.

The way I see it, in reality, is if you can't have perfection in one person, then it is possible to have a series of very close intimate partners of friendship and sex. The sum total of all of them produces what a fantasy image would be. We're talking about where they are intellectually gratifying to me, emotionally stimulating, and sexually exciting, at the same time as being good friends. So what I do in reality is find a piece of somebody in the group. And I am one who has repeated contact. The people I go to bed with have been going on for ten to fifteen years, all over the world. Even if I see them only twice a year, it still occurs.

I have enjoyed myself for a long, long time. I really am not an unhappy person. I like my own company. I find a great deal of pleasure in reading. I have a lot of people I know. I don't have any problems on that score.

If there's one thing that will drive me up the wall, it's a sensation of not being in control. I will not tolerate the sensation of beginning to feel inebriated. Now I mention this to you because I have a tendency to put on weight and I have to go on a diet again. About ten years ago I was given some diet pills, and I found the sensation infuriating. I found myself fighting the sensation of losing control. I don't like to be intoxicated, I have a fear of losing control, by drugs or anything else.

I remember once someone put some amyl nitrate under my nose, but I didn't know what it was, and I could feel the sensation. My reaction to it was not one of pleasure. It was one of intense fury. I flailed out to strike the person who had forced the stuff in my face. I was absolutely livid, which was probably one of the most violent displays of temper that I can remember.

Chapter 14

Kevin
Ex-seminarian with a priest-lover

Kevin is a 35 year old middle-level manager for the electric company. He was born in the Midwest in 1944 with parents twenty years different in age, spent several years in a Catholic seminary, and had his first sexual experience with a married man in the mid-1960s. He has been living for the past nine years with a Catholic priest in a secure and happy relationship. A theme that recurs in Kevin's stories is his genuine concern for other people and the enjoyment he gets out of his life.

FAMILY MEMORIES

My father died when I was a senior in college. He was Italian and had a quick temper, like I do. But he was always pretty reasonable. His parents died and he and his older sister raised the rest of the children. So he didn't marry until he was 38. He was very much respected by his brothers and sisters. I always had good impressions of him. I guess he was what you would call a good family man. He loved his family, he was Italian about that. He was interested in what we did. Sometimes he might not agree, and had a quick temper about that, but it always settled down and you could work it out. When he died, I missed him. He was proud that I went to college. I was the first child out of the family that graduated from college.

He went to college for two years to be a history teacher. He had a good sense of history. When I got into college he always enjoyed talking about it when I was studying history and he was pretty good at it. He remembered quite a bit about what I was studying.

He was a good student even though he didn't get a chance to finish. He liked to read and he liked to study and I have that trait very much. He liked to work with his hands. When I needed a darkroom when I was interested in photography he built a darkroom, and that kind of thing. I'm very much the same way. I like to work with my hands after sitting at a desk for a while. I like to do something, see something done. He was very much the same way.

My mother is quite a bit different. My mother's changed an awful lot since my father died. She had to pretty well come out on her own. When my father died I went to school and my brother was married, so very quickly her house was empty. It was very hard on her. She's made a lot of changes. She's kind of stood up and become her own person a lot more than I think she ever had to before. She always let Dad take care of everything or she didn't worry about it. She didn't know how to pay a bill. She was worried about how to shop for groceries and the typical things that were important to her in her home.

When everybody was gone it was a real devastation for her. But she remarried about five years later. She was worthless for two or three years to herself, and it was a very difficult time getting her to get out and look for a world out there for herself again. She's done that, she's done very well, I'm surprised at just how well she's doing. She's remarried, they have a nice life, she comes and visits. So she's picked up and done very well for herself, under what looked like impossible circumstances.

You would notice very quickly that she doesn't like strangers. When she's introduced and knows your friends or someone that she may have worked or met, that's fine, but she's very much a private person. She doesn't do well with big crowds around or warm up well to strange people when there are large numbers of them. She likes to cook. She likes homespun things, she doesn't like to go out. She'd rather have people at home and have a dinner or something like that rather than to go out places. She's not comfortable out in public places at all. That's probably the biggest characteristic.

I probably have the same general characteristics. I don't like crowds or impersonal parties. I am more comfortable with people in small groups. I'm not as uncomfortable in public as she is. But I prefer if I am going to meet and talk with people I'd rather not be out someplace, I'd rather be home with a group with two, three, four people in it—in a party or dinner—rather than being out in large gatherings.

There was no doubt that my parents were both very much in love. They had problems. I think one of the problems that caused the most difficulty was that Mom left home at such an early age, and probably part of it was just to get out of the house. But in spite of that fact, no matter what problems they had, they were together and that's the way it was. And they worked them out. And I suppose that's the real world. Maybe she was expecting more Hollywood and it wasn't that way. I think she felt that she left and got married too soon. Maybe she should have had a little bit of free life or something like that. But in later yea. s, in retrospect, that attitude worked itself out. I think she just felt that everyone kind of looks for things that could be different if only this, only that, and I think finally she realized that's just the way things were.

EARLY SOCIAL EXPERIENCES

I was interested in the religious life from a young age. I'm a very thoughtful person. I love to read, say, philosophy and sit back and think about questions and things. And that's always been my nature. But I just felt that I could do a lot more outside of the structure which was so rigid.

When I was out teaching school for a while, another seminarian and myself started the first teachers' union that got recognized. Since we knew the politics of the inner circle and how it operates we felt a lot of money came in that was just spent in the wrong way. A $50,000 bell tower is hardly justified when they're paying working people $5,000 and $6,000 a year to teach in their schools. This kind of thing. In other words, the kind of attitude we had some people might not call religious.

The kinds of things I believed and wanted to do were too difficult for me to do because of political pressure that could be put on me. So I just decided that I could do as much outside. People listened to me more when I came back than sometimes from the outside. I just felt a little better that my lifestyle matched my belief, not being in the clerical garb.

I had felt that the job was very much suited to me. In a sense I might say I never left, because I think I do as many things now, in terms of working with people, as I have ever done. And especially with priests. Because I know their rectory environment, I know the pressure and so on, and I also know the experience in the real world, as we call it, out earning a living. There's quite a difference in attitude that it makes. And I've always used that and have been close to a lot of people and have always felt very much in that same circle.

I can't remember being much different from other kids. I was out all day long, I remember that. I wish I had the same energy now that I had then. I mean I could go from sun-up to sundown running and playing athletics. I liked some sports better than others. And I would play, but I also liked to read. I especially liked science when I was young. I played a musical instrument when I was in grade school, maybe sixth grade. I played the sax and clarinet.

EARLY SEXUAL MEMORIES

Ever since I can remember, I always favored men. But as far as sexual experience, it was not until I was in high school or the first year in college. I masturbated very infrequently, on a few, difficult to remember occasions. Not much sexual experience until somewhere in college and I'm trying to think if it may have been later than freshman year. So, definitely in the early 1960s, when I was in my 20s. But I had always, since any time I can remember, felt more inclined towards males. Never a heterosexual experience. Never an inclination toward females at all.

I was depressed when I felt I was gay and pretending to be straight. I really felt bad, just like it was no place for me. But somewhere along the line, I said that's what you've got and that's what you're going to have to live with. And that was it. But I was very, very depressed at that time.

I went to confession maybe a couple of times and considered it mostly hopeless insofar as I don't think that the priest really knew what was going on nor that he could handle it. I guess I was an independent thinker because I just realized that somebody's just off base and I just realized that wasn't where it was. Ever since I could remember I was gay and that's the way I was. And I just couldn't take all the moral condemnation. I just couldn't buy it that way. So that somewhere I had to work it out. You just kind of had to stand up against everything that was; just do something and find a place for yourself or there wasn't going to be one.

The first sexual experience that I can remember was with someone that I had known for a long time. He was a married man. I was at a party and I wasn't feeling very well, so I went upstairs and laid down. And he came upstairs and that was the first sexual experience that I've ever had. I was probably somewhere in my early 20s. He just laid on the bed next to me. I'd known him for ten years. I knew the whole family, all the brothers and sisters, it was a large family. And always they had been very good to me. I always went to everything, known them for years, went to school with some of them. And so we were always very close in that regard. And he came upstairs and laid down next to me and just kind of hugged me and went down on me. And never really saying anything. I guess that kind of unspoken thing that just goes between people. It kind of surprised me. I didn't really know that he was gay, because he was married and had four or five kids. Always talking about girls. The typical remarks that might go on and that kind of thing. So that in a sense I thought he always horsed around a lot, but I'd never really thought he was gay. It was surprising. He was very upset and I was just kind of surprised. And I later told him not to be upset about it because it didn't upset me. And that was all that we said, he'd gone back to the party.

I guess he was acting under the pretense that he'd had maybe something too much to drink, which really wasn't the case. And I told him there was nothing to be upset about. We had been close friends and it was kind of a sense of closeness expressed physically that didn't upset me. And we have been very good friends ever since.

Most of my friends at that time were straight. As far as gay friends, I didn't have a whole lot, maybe three or four. When I went to college I had met a few other people who were gay, but eventually I met the person with whom I've lived for the last nine years. And we met in college.

CURRENT SITUATION AND EXPERIENCE

My relationship has been great. When you think of the problems that you have to overcome, the feeling of isolation, the fact that you just don't go out and tell everybody that you're gay. Even in your job, I don't think you'll find too many gays who work in a position that I do. They must have a way of keeping it to a minimum, at least in the management jobs.

At a certain point you have to decide who you are, what you are, and you just take what you've got and go with it. And that's very much what we've done. In the nine years we've had a very good relationship. It's been a foundation for both of us to feel pretty secure and because of it I've never worried in my office. You just feel kind of secure. You know you have your home and you're happy, you just don't have to worry what other people say or think, it just kind of changes your whole outlook. We have very few difficulties.

The first year we were together, we kind of decided that everybody had their own little habits and things and if you get mad or annoyed, that it couldn't last at night. Then by the time it was time to go to bed everything had to be over with. And it was and it has been ever since. We had a major problem or disagreement years on down the road. It's hard to say just what the problem was. But whatever it was, the bottom line came out: I'm not leaving and you're not leaving, we're together, we're very much in love with each other. We always work things out. In a period of years you take a lot of things for granted, start getting into routines, at times you just have to break away from it. I have a need to be more with him and nothing else seems to make as much difference. I've grown closer or more attached or more involved with him over the years, and the physical expression of it is much deeper.

I should say that my lover is a priest. The only problem has been that we tended to be very discreet, in terms of not just flaunting ourselves out and around. But we really found out that there wasn't any problems. He has his professional interests he has to take care of and I have a different group that I have to cater to. If you have to go to an office party once in a while or something of that nature, we have that to attend to sometimes.

Being gay makes you very independent. You just have to stand up because most of the cards are stacked against you, in people's attitudes and society in general. And if you can find out who you are and what you are, you're going to have to do it fast. It's made me put my pieces together fast and say, you know, here's the lemons I got dealt in life and I'm going to make lemonade. And that's the way it's been. So now that I don't consider myself a second-class citizen anymore, I just say I'm another person who's been given what he's been given and this is what I have to do with it. Like it or lump it, right or wrong, I don't know, I just made the best decisions I could, but I'm not just going to take my life and sit with it and go nowhere. And I guess I've been forced to decide that at an early age because of it.

I enjoy a dinner party. I like to go over, meet people. I like to talk to people seriously. I don't like casual talk from my friends. I like to know what they think, what they feel, what's on their minds. That kind of thing. I don't like just idle chat. I tend to like to know people well.

Chapter 15

Louis

Two lovers, many lives

Louis is a 50 year old college professor, born in 1928, who grew up as an only child in Oklahoma. His earliest sexual experiences were with female prostitutes. It wasn't until college that he first started thinking about his homosexuality, but it was in the Army during the early 1950s that he finally acted on it. Louis's current situation is unusual: he divides his love life between a man he has lived with for fourteen years and another man, twenty years younger, whom he has seen regularly for three years, and still finds time for occasional sex with a woman. All are involved socially and in financial partnership. How Louis manages his life and loves is the focus of much of his story.

FAMILY MEMORIES

My father is a generally quiet man. He's an outdoors man, likes to fish and hunt, or used to. Until he retired he raised cattle after owning his own construction business. He's a very gentle, quiet sort of man. Good, quiet sense of humor. We've always been on the best of terms. I have tremendous respect for him. We're terribly good friends.

We've gotten to be better friends I suppose since I was of college age. He always took me fishing with him. He encouraged my school activities. He was always there whenever I needed him, but he never attempted to influence or guide me in any strong way—that is, to follow the profession that he had, or to push me to do something that he thought was important. He always let me make my own decisions.

My personality and intellectual curiosity are like his. I hope so, because he's always been a role model for me. I would always retreat to him whenever I had differences with my mother, and I would always retreat to my mother if I had childhood differences with my father. But I think it was a very even-handed kind of relationship.

He was the ultimate disciplinarian. My mother usually told me what I should do and if I did not do it she would administer any kind of forfeit or punishment. But if it were a major difficulty, my father would be the disciplinarian.

My father always treated her with a great deal of respect. I don't know that I ever recall them having but one or two arguments or disagreements in my presence, and these were times of considerable stress. When we moved, mother was very unhappy at being taken away from her family and friends. I recall that as being one very difficult time. Another time they had moved into the house with my grandmother and grandfather when they moved up to a little town. He very much wanted to move away, she wanted to move away, but they felt they couldn't, and it was a difficult situation. But those are the only two times I can recall any kind of argument or words of any decibels.

We were a very touchy family. Much physical reassurance, hugging, patting, and both my mother and father equally. I used to sit on my father's lap a great deal. My mother was always very demonstrative.

I think my father's somewhat Victorian sexually. He was the youngest of three sons and was very close to his mother and she was very Yankee and very Victorian. Intellectually enlightened, but I think, in terms of sexuality, it wasn't something one could talk a great deal about. The facts of life were presented to me by both parents very, very clinically and only upon my own curiosity.

My mother is more outgoing, more social than my father. She loves to entertain. She's a very aware person. She handles people and deals with people so well. Not so much intellectually, but very understanding, very curious, vivacious, not pretty, but a handsome woman. I think she grew up somewhat in the shadow of her older sister, my aunt, who was something of a beauty, and so I think she probably tried to compensate by having personality and warmth. Pretty tremendous woman. And very tough inside.

We have always been very close and have remained so. She was my primary confidante and still is. Anything she asks me I will tell her. My confidence with my father has been in different matters. Our relationship has always been more in terms of what conventionally is men's talk—politics, philosophy, sports, his business interests, my professional interests, people we knew in common, current events. With mother it's always been a little more aesthetically oriented, though my father is not naive in terms of the arts—he's very appreciative. Mother is a lady in every sense. She went to a very good girls' school and with her Southern background that makes her somewhat polished, smooth. I love to see her operate when I bring her East among my friends.

My impression is she was a little more relaxed about sex than my father. Indeed, I suppose you go back to the disposition of the facts of life—hers was a much easier kind of exposition than my father's, so this would be the hint. Also, I think women tend to notice the sexual affairs of their friends and comment upon what the young people are doing these days compared to what they did in her day, and it doesn't seem to offend her. I think my father does sometimes take offense at young people living together and premarital sex.

Physically I resemble her, and I am more social than my father, more outgoing, but it goes in a cycle. When I want company, I want company. And when I don't, I find myself being more like my father. My father is not really an outgoing social person at all. I share a lot of my mother's tastes and a lot of her interests, particularly about, oh, design, cooking, these things—homemaking things. I don't think I consider myself interested in fashion any more than my father, but my mother makes me aware of it.

They have a very good marriage, over fifty years. He was her dress man, and she had dated quite lively. I knew a lot of her beaus, because they still lived in the same town, and theirs was a courtship of about a year, but I think she knew she made a really fine catch, in terms of personality and intelligence, as well as a pretty attractive man.

EARLY SOCIAL EXPERIENCES

I am an only child, but I never perceived it as a problem until after I attained adulthood. I realized that probably I missed something by not having a close association with brothers and sisters. I had a lot of childhood playmates in the neighborhood. My two closest neighbors were both girls, and a few blocks away lived a couple of boys that I grew up with. So my four closest friends were equally divided in sex.

I was the best little boy in the world, in every sense. Being an only child I'm sure I was terribly spoiled, but not even my enemies would say I was a brat because I was pretty well behaved. I had the undivided attention of my parents and my maternal grandparents. My paternal grandparents had other grandchildren, but I would always go down for a week in the summer with my paternal grandmother and grandfather on the farm. We were very close—a very close family.

I got dancing lessons and piano lessons, and usually Christmas was always staged around whatever my whims were. My paternal grandfather loved to take me for walks and riding and we spent a great deal of time together. My grandmother, my maternal grandmother, was really a very bad disciplinarian—she would spoil me with gifts and give me money when she shouldn't have, and take my side in an argument against my parents.

I was perhaps somewhat bashful and shy. And both my mother and father always encouraged me to speak up and go to parties. They gave big birthday parties for me. Mother would always see that I got to those things. I was encouraged to make speeches and take part in church programs and school programs. My father was very interested that I learned how to throw a baseball and a football. I received an awful lot of attention and tutoring to bring me out of the family circle.

I was not interested in sports. I never really liked baseball very much. That was my grandfather's sport, and he would take me to baseball games and I'd be bored stiff—but football captured my attention. My father was a collegiate football player, and quite good. I played tennis, was a member of the high school debate team and theater club.

EARLY SEXUAL MEMORIES

I found out about sex mostly by reading. I was a voracious reader. Both my mother and father encouraged me in this. I think it was a fairly early puberty. I know I began to develop secondary male characteristics before the other boys on my block.

I had difficulty deciding which side of the sexual street I was going to spend most of my time on. I had dated girls in high school and went through petting. In terms of college, this also was the activity. I dated several girls in college and we had "made out" as the term was then, without having fully consummated the sex act.

One of my friends and I used to go off to the local massage parlor, which was a private bar and a house of prostitution, on Wednesday afternoon after class. Another friend of mine introduced me to this chicken ranch, like the one in the Broadway musical. We used to go there at homecoming games and when I was visiting them down there. But most of my purely physical sex life was either at pickups or among prostitutes. I did have a couple of dates.

No homosexual activity as an undergraduate, at all. I did have a couple of girls that I dated steadily. Ultimately we went to bed together, and it was usually their initiation rather than mine. I'm not aggressive sexually. Maybe it was the bad company I kept that enabled me to get off with prostitutes, but with nice girls I would usually let them make the advances, except for this one girl that I found extremely attractive. I pushed my luck and kept winning with her, but I didn't begin to get curious about the alternative until I was, I suppose, a junior or senior in college. This would be right after the war in the late '40s. And I began noticing that there was a very compatible beauty about my fraternity brothers as well. Of course, I wouldn't touch any of them, or even bring it up with any of them.

I had fantasized about males. And I found that my attitude toward male beauty was very different from that of my other friends. One of the single points that alerted me to the fact that my attention was more than purely aesthetic is that one year I was rush chairman for the fraternity and we had an extremely successful rush year. I was just sitting there looking at our pledge class and I thought, my God, did we ever catch a bunch of beauties. I said that to myself, and when I said it, it sort of clicked a bell, and I thought that's how you really think of them, isn't it? As beauties. And so, that began to make me think about it.

This was about the time I was a junior in college. There were a couple of guys in the fraternity that I had heard talk about and I knew they were gay, and I enjoyed them. They were witty, they were fun. They were doing things other people weren't doing, and they would run off to Mexico together and I guess carry on a kind of restrained camp even with the other guys. I found them fascinating and became very good friends. One of the guys in the fraternity was the town sissy, but his father had been a very important member of the fraternity. I really thought he would be bad news for the group, but since his father prevailed upon us to pledge him, we did and I became his big brother and tried to put long pants on him, as it were. We became very good friends, as a matter of fact.

I had another crush on another fraternity brother who was younger than I was. I was his big brother, and I thought he was tremendously interesting. I learned to love baseball because of him. He was terribly square and terribly straight, but an absolutely terrific guy. He was cute and funny and fun to be with and we double dated a great deal.

My college roommate in undergraduate school was also someone who I realized I was sexually attracted to. We were good friends but sex never came up. We roomed together, we double dated together, horsed around a great deal together, but no physical consummation, not so much as even a kiss. I was physically attracted to my college roommate. That's one of the reasons I wanted to room with him, because I enjoyed looking at him and being with him. He also had some characteristics that I hoped I could acquire.

I also had what was probably a terribly physical attraction to a kid I was tutoring who wasn't a member of our fraternity at all. He was on the basketball team. I would help him with his term papers. He lived in the dorm, and I would see him two or three evenings a week. I'd go to basketball practice just to watch him, because he was not only a terribly sweet guy who needed a lot of help to stay in school, but he was also a strikingly beautiful man. He reciprocated in terms of "oh gosh", toe-in-the-sand kind of affection. What I realized was happening was that he was beginning to like me too much for the wrong reasons, because after the team won, he came out of the locker room and gave me a great big hug and lifted me up.

There were a couple of situations in school at that time—a couple of bars that were questionable—and I'd heard about them. I went there on my own, and I was picked up there once upon a time. But the result was really not very satisfactory and I'm sure I was scared about it—so scared indeed that I never went back there again.

I guess it was only in the Army in the early '50s that I really began to experiment. At band school there were a lot of musicians—and a lot of people from other backgrounds—and some of them carried on outrageously. Being among musicians in the Army I increased my knowledge and familiarity with gay life considerably. I suppose it was only on my leaves that I began experimenting with other men and found it extremely satisfactory. More stimulating. More physically satisfying afterwards. I got off both ways, but the pleasure and enjoyment was great with men. Indeed, at one time I was dating a German girl and a German boy at the same time in Munich, and I just found I was seeing more and more of him and less and less of her.

I knew homosexuality could present a lot of problems, and I didn't talk to anybody about it because I figured this was a matter I'd have to work out on my own. But I wasn't so afraid of it that I didn't continue to experiment with it. And I really didn't play around that much while I was in Europe. I did establish a very nice relationship with a German fellow in Munich and I found myself toward the end of my tour beginning to seek out homosexual bars and homosexual contacts on my leaves.

While I was in the Army one of my very close friends in college was also in the Army on leave and he had a motorcycle. We went to Paris together and we met again in Venice, and I realized for the first time that I sort of had a physical crush on him too, but I made no overtures because of our long-standing background.

When I came back from the Army in 1955 and started my Masters work, I was about 26, I was really beginning to look at the guys in a very different light. By that time I found that another one of my fraternity brothers was gay. I knew he was gay, but he didn't know I was. I never broached the subject with him until he ran into me in a bar in New York.

An interesting thing in my graduate school experience happened. I had a couple of introductory courses which I was fully responsible for, and there was a young man in one of them who I found attractive. He was a track star, local radio announcer, big wheel in his fraternity. He was an undergraduate and I was a graduate student and we developed a very good friendship. I gave him a "D" in the course. It was the first "D" he had ever gotten. He wanted to talk about it so we met after his evening DJ program on the local radio station, and suddenly decided we liked each other a lot. He was a blatant heterosexual—even a satyrist I found out later. But we really hit it off very well and so he moved out of the fraternity house and we shared an apartment while I was finishing graduate school. The house that we had had only one double bed and we slept together. No sexual activity at all, but I had a tremendous physical attraction to him. He was athletic, he was young, he was vivacious and bright and very funny.

So I tutored him and was best man at his wedding and he went off to become a CIA agent and eventually worked in publishing. His wife divorced him because she found out he was carrying on with three other women on the side. A very, very interesting guy. That was sort of a platonic affair that did have sexual overtones on my part.

Then I moved to New York. I really began trying to find out what the gay world was like. Still somewhat limited, a couple of bars on the East side, maybe one in the Village, I did a lot of street cruising and at that time would never have thought about going to the baths but I'd heard about them. From about 1960 to 1964/5 I was a young single professional who really tried to find out as much as I could about this world that I'd heard about.

I made it a rule, because at that time I was concerned about professional involvement and wasn't really sure I wanted to opt for being a lifetime homosexual, so I would hardly see anyone more than two or three times at the most and then I would automatically break off the relationship. I thought it would be stupid to see people only once, particularly if you enjoyed each other, but if it looked like it was going to blossom into something that might smack of commitment or might smack of labeling I would drop it.

I had two affairs. One guy I met in a bar and he was the president of a bank. We had a very passionate short affair. Took our vacation together, spent several long weekends at his parents' house. We dated on and off for I guess six months or so, and I realized that he was getting too serious about it. I realized it was not going to be comfortable for him to find it interesting too much longer. We're still friends. We still exchange Christmas cards and we still see each other once or twice a year.

The other affair was with an 18 year old Cuban, but because of distance and because of difference in ages, it ended. He was about as afraid of a long-term relationship, he did not want one, I did not either, but we also are good friends to this day.

Then one night, I went out to mail a letter and stopped in a bar. There was one other individual in there who was a tall, blue-eyed blond—the most incredible blond hair I'd ever seen—and I bought him a beer and he bought me a beer. We played the records, some other people came in, and I took him home with me. He was here on a buying trip from the Midwest for a major department store. It was really the first time I had fallen for anybody emotionally. We spent Tuesday night together, he had a date on Wednesday night. We spent Thursday, Friday, Saturday—the Labor Day weekend—went out to Fire Island with a couple of gay friends. He called me back as soon as he arrived back home and I realized something important was going on. For a year I went to the Midwest one month and he would come here one month. The airlines and phone company profited! I went out and spent a summer with him at a lake house that a good friend of ours had and we decided that this commuting was foolish and he should move to New Jersey. This was August of '65, and the following January he moved here and we've been lovers for almost fourteen years.

CURRENT SITUATION AND EXPERIENCES

For the last fourteen years up until the last two years, I suppose we were considered the ideal relationship. In fact we really never had an argument until four years ago. We had a large circle of friends and entertained quite a lot. We saw most of the theater and art openings. We were invited away on weekends with some regularity. A large composite of mutual friends.

Our sex was quite satisfactory, tending to be affectionate and ostensibly monogamous—but we both knew a little better, but we didn't say anything about it. That was the arrangement. We both were aware of it, but we pretended it did not exist. It was something you didn't discuss with your mate, and we were far more circumspect I guess than most of our friends were. And that worked out pretty well.

The last couple of years he's had some professional difficulties, having a hard time finding a regular job. This has eaten into his financial resources and he's made some difficult adjustments, particularly because we had committed ourselves in a partnership to buy property together.

He's ten years younger than I am. He's extremely creative, a very handsome guy. In some respects he reminds me of my father. As I say, we are still lovers. The last couple or three years have been difficult, primarily because of his situation, and primarily because we decided to be honest with each other about our extracurricular physical activities.

Three years ago I met another guy through business contacts and we realized that we also had something very much in common. Mark is twenty years younger and he has become my best friend. Now my lover, David, and I have the property together and a long-term relationship that is still quite solid and quite good. My best friend and I are partners in a house that he and his lover and my lover and I have bought together. He bought the house a little over a year ago. Our objective was that we would put it in my best friend's name and my own, primarily for tax purposes, but in terms of ownership, it's owned by four partners—legally it's owned by two partners.

I also am involved sexually with my best friend. Maybe once or twice a month. It started out being quite a mental trip. He's an unusual man in many ways too—creative and very philosophical and very wild in terms of his background. He's a Vietnam veteran. I'd never smoked a joint until I met him and he turned me on. He liked drugs and smoking and a whole lot different lifestyle.

It started out mental, it got physical, and in a sense we are in business together. We have a product that we're manufacturing and selling as a sideline, and we see each other three or four times a week at breakfast or business, and usually maybe one night every week we'll go out socially on a date. He and my lover are fairly good friends as well. I've been accused of having two lovers, but I don't think my best friend would call it that because he has a lover. However, he doesn't have sex with his lover anymore but he has sex with me about once every couple of weeks or so.

It has required a very difficult adjustment, because while my lover says he's not, I know he's terribly jealous of our relationship. I've encouraged him to have some friends as well. He has a couple of friends he enjoys who maybe he'll go out with, both of whom are younger than he. I thought that would be a healthy thing because he being the junior partner in our relationship so far as knowledge, and certainly the junior partner with his bad business life, he needed to play a more mature role with a younger man as a bigger brother. I thought that would give him some satisfaction, and some sense of responsibility.

When we got together, my lover David said, "Why don't I just give you all of my money—you take care of the books and we'll just make one pot." I resisted that for a couple of reasons. One was that he who keeps the finances also exerts control, and I did not want a man who was ten years my junior coming to me wanting an allowance. My feeling was he needed to manage his own affairs to keep self-respect and responsibility, and so I nixed that. So we have split everything right down the middle in terms of expenditures, except where it is a capital improvement and this we try to do on a proportionate income. My income is larger than his so I would pay a larger share. For luxury things I would pay a larger share. In the last year it has been quite difficult because I've had to pay most of the share because of his income.

I am beginning to feel that it is an imposition, and what it has done is interfere with the same lifestyle he's trying to protect. I know he's desperately trying to find other sources of income, and I encourage him in this. I will not drop him for financial reasons, but I sometimes get the feeling that maybe he is leaning on me too heavily about trying hard enough.

We still have sex together. There was a hiatus of about four months earlier in the year and then a hiatus of about one month. It was a period of economic adjustment and his getting used to the idea that my friend is a permanent part of the arrangement. He is getting used to the idea. He planned my 50th birthday party in conjunction with my best friend. My best friend arranged for all the champagne and everything here, and they both took me to the party under the ruse of going to a friend's house for drinks. It was jointly their project on my behalf and they both took me home and they both took me to bed, a three-way, so it was a lovely birthday.

Initially my best friend Mark had cruised and tried to pick up my lover David before he met me. And he did not know David and I were lovers. I had been seeing my best friend on and off circumspectly. His relationship had been open for a long while; both he and his lover were seeing other people, dating each other, spending the night out, and they viewed it as a kind of maturity. One afternoon at the office I picked up the phone and it was Mark and he said, "Say, your lover knows my lover," and I said, "What do you mean?" He said, "Well, I was describing to my lover your apartment, tile floors, the fireplace, and he looked at me and said, 'Aren't there large floor lamps in the back bedroom?', and I said, 'Yes', and he said, 'My lover knows your lover and has seen him a couple of times'."

Then, he said, "You two should really come clean with each other. You both know that you have been playing around and particularly at this stage in your relationship you should be able to withstand complete openness. If you want to see other people besides each other you should do so. You should be mature enough to do so."

One night after my lover said he got VD from someone else, we sat down and admitted to each other that we had carried on when we said we had not. We filled in some informational gaps, and I said that I knew that he had seen my friend's friend a couple of times and that I thought he should know that I was seeing the guy's lover that he had seen and that we were very good friends. So we got to know each other socially, we invited them both. My lover gets along very well with my good friend, who does not get along so well with his lover, and vice versa.

I would never break off our relationship. I don't think he would either. I would not think it was because of economic dependence on me at this time. Back from Christmas holiday we had a very good long weekend together, several times, and talked out a lot of problems, and I do see us as a future because he gives me things and stimulates me in ways that nobody else does. His sensitivity, his creativity, his outgoing kind of socialness is a very important adjunct to me. I know a whole different aspect of life knowing somebody like him. He's good emotional support, though I think probably I offer him more emotional support at this time than he offers me.

It's become an affectation of mine to go to the baths in the last five years or so. Before David and I became open with each other I would sneak off when he was out of town on business or in the afternoon. And I enjoyed that. It's good recreation. To me there are three kinds of sex: there's one that's passionate and loving; there's one of communication, which is an extension of friendship and tactile communication; and there's recreational sex, where you do it for the fun of it to make your fantasies come alive, and that's the function of baths.

Also, about once a year, I'll have sex with a woman, whether I need it or not, just to keep my hand in, but not to reassure myself of my masculinity. I get off on having guys turned on to me much more than girls. I don't like to think of myself as being exclusively appreciative of people. I find some women extremely attractive and maybe twice a year—anyhow, I'll probably go out and cruise a singles bar and take home a girl. I have a couple of gay girlfriends that I sleep with occasionally. They're curious sometimes and enjoy it and I do as well. One of them has been married before. I enjoy the female body a great deal. The female bodies that I find most attractive are the long, lean bony types that reflect a lot about what I find attractive in male bodies.

My family has never asked me. But I have a feeling that they are aware I'm gay. My policy has always been that if they ever ask me a direct question, they, I assume, would be ready for an answer. Then I would be perfectly frank and tell them. But I assume that they're not going to ask me because they don't want to know in hard words. They have met my lover on their visits here. He's visited with my family and me twice. When they came up the time before last we were scheduled to have a cocktail party. Socially we mix with straight as well as gay couples, and among gay couples we always have some rather attractive lady gay couples—lesbians. When people come in we just explained to them that they could kiss anybody but their lovers, or of the same sex, and all of my friends were aware that my parents were not aware. My parents enjoyed them tremendously, and both the gay and straight friends ask about my parents and my parents ask about different people they have met.

I know that at least three members of my department are gay, either by first-hand reputation or I have seen them in situations that leave no doubt, but I've never discussed it with my colleagues. When I was Department Chairman I had my lover come by to help me do something with the office. Since my best friend is my business partner, he frequently came to the office and we would use my office for business purposes, conferences, and so on. I really don't know what my colleagues think. I would assume most of them being New Yorkers would be reasonably sophisticated enough to assume that I was gay.

I'm really a very introspective kind of person. And one of the things that I think that's made my life so terribly pleasant is that I've always found friends who were interested in talking about me and about them, and it is one of the bonds between me and my best friend. We probe each other's psyches, and try to challenge each other to justify why we have a certain attitude, why we feel or think as we do.

About once a year, I'll go through my periodic black mood, and I will get very frustrated because I can't immediately accomplish all the things that I feel I should accomplish. I'll get depressed because I think I've got too much work, too little time to do it, because I'm not doing as good a job as I think I would like to do. And I'll get frustrated because I'm of the opinion I can do nothing about it. So I'll withdraw for maybe a day or two.

I'm terribly pleased to have gotten to be 50 with no major mishaps, physical or financial. I like my job pretty well. I'm less satisfied with it, I'm getting bored with the subject. I've done about what I want to do in it. I'm more interested in real estate and more interested in this business adventure, so professionally, let's say I've not achieved my goals but I have achieved limited objectives.

I am very anxious that David get on his feet psychologically and economically because it is bothering him, personality wise. I love him very much. And I would want us still to be together. My best friend and I, I would like to see our business venture blossom together. We certainly need each other, I hope we are still best friends then, and that may or may not happen in either case. Death, accident, emotional upheaval, all of these things are possibilities, but if I had my way I would like to see my immediate personal life continue pretty much as it is.

I'm not religious in the organized sense. Unitarianism represented a kind of movement toward freedom of religious thought and philosophy for me, and rationalized perhaps a lot of the things that I found objectionable about the Protestant religion. I've always been something of a skeptic and Unitarianism offered me intellectual as well as a moral justification for it. I think I really followed my father's line of thinking, who was more of a deist than anything else, and very close to nature and natural phenomena. And a good many of my friends who would deny they are religious but do have a philosophical bent are some of my closest friends. And I like to think that I'm a fairly moral person, a continuous searcher.

Because I am gay I've had a much fuller life so far than most of my straight contemporaries that I know well. My range of experience, contact, the freedom to travel, the freedom to see things, do things, the lack of family responsibility, the encouragement of my gay friends to do things that I probably would not have done, plus the range of acquaintances. I have very good friends in their 70s that are gay; I have a couple of very good friends in their early 20s that are gay, and I don't know any straight guys that have friends over that chronological range. I also don't know many straight men who have such close friends as I have—my best friend and a couple of other people—and I think this has been particularly enriching. The freedom, the range of exposure, the range of intellect, moving in different circles—all of these have been pluses, in spades, as far as I'm concerned.

The only real disadvantage, and I think that sometimes it does bother me, is that I haven't provided grandchildren for my parents because I think that's something that they would have wanted. But that is nothing that I can do anything about, and so I don't feel guilty about it. I have come to believe that they would want grandchildren more for status and acceptance in their circle than that they really would have enjoyed them as people, because they're really not that fond of children. Perhaps this is a rationalization; if they were really crazy about kids, why didn't they have more than one anyhow?

I had a neighbor once confront me at the dinner table—she'd been invited to dinner one night—and we were sitting around and she confronted me, "Aren't you ashamed of yourself not carrying on the family name? Everyone thinks it's just terrible that your mother and father don't have grandchildren like everybody else." And I was really taken aback that anybody would confront me on my own turf with that kind of personal question. I collected myself and said, "I'm really surprised that you'd ask that kind of question since it apparently, and obviously, is none of your business." And we just dropped it at that.

References

Adam, B. D. (1987) *The Rise of a Gay and Lesbian Movement*, Boston: Twayne.
Bayer, R. (1981) *Homosexuality and American Psychiatry*, New York: Basic Books.
Bell, A., Weinberg, M. and Hammersmith, S. K. (1981) *Sexual Preference: Its Development in Men and Women*, Bloomington: Indiana University Press.
Berger, P. (1963) *Invitation to Sociology: A Humanistic Perspective*, Garden City, NY: Anchor Doubleday.
Bergler, E. (1951) *Counterfeit Sex*, New York: Grune & Stratton.
Berube, A. (1990) *Coming Out Under Fire: The History of Gay Men and Women in World War Two*, New York: Free Press.
Bieber, I., Dain, H., Dince, P., Drellich, M., Grand, H., Gundlach, R., Kremer, M., Rifkin, A., Wilbur, C. and Bieber, T. (1962) *Homosexuality: A Psychoanalytic Study*, New York: Basic Books.
Blum, R. (1981) "Psychological processes in preparing contemporary biography," *Biography* 4: 293–311.
Brown, H. (1976) *Familiar Faces, Hidden Lives: The Story of Homosexual Men in America Today*, New York: Harcourt Brace Jovanovich.
Chauncey, Jr., G. (1985) "Christian brotherhood or sexual perversion? Homosexual identities and the construction of sexual boundaries in the World War I era," *Journal of Social History* 19: 189–212.
Connell, R. W. (1992) "A very straight gay: masculinity, homosexual experience, and the dynamics of gender," *American Sociological Review* 57: 735–51.
Cory, D. W. (1951) *The Homosexual in America*, New York: Paperback Library Inc.
Crowley, M. (1968) *The Boys in the Band*, New York: Dell.
Davison, G. C. (1991) "Constructionism and morality in therapy for homosexuality," in J. Gonsiorek and J. Weinrich (eds.) *Homosexuality: Research Implications for Public Policy*, Newbury Park, CA: Sage.
D'Emilio, J. (1983) *Sexual Politics, Sexual Communities*, Chicago: University of Chicago Press.
Duberman, M. (1991) *Cures: A Gay Man's Odyssey*, New York: Dutton.
Faderman, L. (1991) *Odd Girls and Twilight Lovers: A History of Lesbian Life in Twentieth-Century America*, New York: Penguin.
Freeman, J. and Krantz, D. (1980) "The unfulfilled promise of life histories," *Biography* 3: 1–13.

Freud, A. (1949) "Some clinical remarks concerning the treatment of cases of male homosexuality," *International Journal of Psychoanalysis* 30: 195.

Gubrium, J. and Buckholdt, D. (1977) *Toward Maturity*, San Francisco: Jossey-Bass.

Hadden, S. B. (1966) "Treatment of male homosexuals in groups," *International Journal of Group Psychotherapy* 16: 13–22.

Haldeman, D. C. (1991) "Sexual orientation conversion therapy for gay men and lesbians: A scientific examination," in J. Gonsiorek and J. Weinrich (eds.) *Homosexuality: Research Implications for Public Policy*, Newbury Park, CA: Sage.

Hall Carpenter Archives (1989a) *Inventing Ourselves: Lesbian Life Stories*, London: Routledge.

—— (1989b) *Walking After Midnight: Gay Men's Life Stories*, London: Routledge.

Hatterer, L. J. (1970) *Changing Homosexuality in the Male*, New York: McGraw-Hill.

Hooker, E. (1957) "The adjustment of the male overt homosexual," *Journal of Projective Techniques* 21: 17–31.

Kolb, L. C. and Johnson, A. M. (1955) "Etiology and therapy of overt homosexuality," *Psychoanalytic Quarterly* 24: 506–15.

Marmor, J. (ed.) (1965) *Sexual Inversion: The Multiple Roots of Homosexuality*, New York: Basic Books.

—— (ed.) (1980) *Homosexual Behavior: A Modern Reappraisal*, New York: Basic Books.

McAdam, D. P. (1985) *Power, Intimacy, and the Life Story: Personological Inquiries into Identity*, Homewood, IL: Dorsey.

Nardi, P. M. (1992) "That's what friends are for: Friends as family in the gay and lesbian community," in K. Plummer (ed.), *Modern Homosexualities: Fragments of Lesbian and Gay Experience*, London: Routledge.

Ovesey, L. (1965) "Psuedohomosexuality and homosexuality in men: Psychodynamics as a guide to treatment," in J. Marmor (ed.) *Sexual Inversion: The Multiple Roots of Homosexuality*, New York: Basic Books.

Plummer, K. (1983) *Documents of Life*, London: Allen & Unwin.

Porter, K. and Weeks, J. (eds.) (1991) *Between the Acts: Lives of Homosexual Men 1885–1967*, London: Routledge.

Rodgers, B. (1972) *Gay Talk [The Queens" Vernacular]*, New York: Paragon.

Ross, M. W. (1980) "Retrospective distortion in homosexual research," *Archives of Sexual Behavior* 9: 523–31.

Sanders, D. S. (1980) "A psychotherapeutic approach to homosexual men," in J. Marmor (ed.) *Homosexual Behavior: A Modern Reappraisal*, New York: Basic Books.

Siegelman, M. (1974) "Parental background of male homosexuals and heterosexuals," *Archives of Sexual Behavior* 6: 3–18.

Socarides, C. (1968) *The Overt Homosexual*, New York: Grune & Stratton.

Warren, C. (1974) *Identity and Community in the Gay World*, New York: Wiley.

Welch, P. (1964) "Homosexuality in America: The 'gay' world takes to the city streets," *Life* June 26: 66–74.

Weston, K. (1991) *Families We Choose: Lesbians, Gays, Kinship*, New York: Columbia University Press.

Name index